Foreign National Asset-Based Mortgage Loans

How International Buyers Qualify for U.S. Mortgage Loans Using Global Assets

By Joseph G. Correa

Licensed Mortgage Broker, Finibi Mortgage

Copyright & Legal Notice

Published by Live Stronger Faster

The information provided in this book is for educational and informational purposes only and does not constitute financial, legal, tax, or investment advice. The author and publisher make no representations or warranties regarding the accuracy, completeness, or applicability of the content. Readers are encouraged to consult with licensed professionals, including mortgage lenders, financial advisors, tax professionals, and attorneys, before making any financial decisions.

The strategies and examples discussed in this book are illustrative in nature and may not be suitable for all individuals or situations. Results may vary based on market conditions, lender guidelines, and individual financial circumstances. The author and publisher are not responsible for any financial losses, decisions, or outcomes resulting from the use or misuse of the information contained in this book.

First Edition, 2026

Table of Contents

Foreword 6

Chapter 1: Understanding Foreign National Asset-Based Mortgage Lending........ 12

Chapter 2: Structuring and Documenting Global Assets for Mortgage Approval........ 21

Chapter 3: Risk Assessment, Lender Overlays, and Strategic Positioning for Approval........ 31

Chapter 4: Loan Programs, Terms, and Structuring Options for Foreign National Borrowers........ 40

Chapter 5: Navigating the Loan Process, Timelines, and Closing Strategies for Foreign National Borrowers........ 49

Chapter 6: Scaling a U.S. Real Estate Portfolio as a Foreign National Using Asset-Based Financing........57

Chapter 7: Exit Strategies, Refinancing, and Long-Term Wealth Optimization for Foreign National Borrowers........ 65

Chapter 8: Advanced Portfolio Optimization, Global Structuring, and Legacy Wealth Strategies for Foreign National Investors........73

Chapter 9: Risk Mitigation, Compliance, and Protecting Your Global Real Estate Investments........ 81

Chapter 10: Building a Global Real Estate Empire with Asset-Based Mortgage Strategies.. 89

Chapter 11: Building Systems, Automation, and a Self-Sustaining Real Estate Machine.................................... 97

Chapter 12: Mastery, Control, and the Long-Term Evolution of a Global Asset-Based Real Estate Strategy.......................... 105

Chapter 13: Advanced Deal Structuring, Creative Financing, and Unlocking Hidden Opportunities................................. 113

Chapter 14: Creating Predictable Deal Flow, Building Strategic Partnerships, and Operating at Scale.................................. 120

Chapter 15: The Ultimate Wealth Flywheel—Compounding Assets, Capital, and Control Over Time............................... 128

Final Thoughts... 135

Foreword

In today's increasingly globalized world, real estate ownership is no longer confined by borders. Wealth, opportunity, and capital flow across countries at a speed and scale never seen before, and with that shift comes a powerful question: how can international buyers access real estate opportunities in the United States without relying on traditional income verification within the U.S. system? This book was created to answer that question in a clear, strategic, and empowering way. Welcome to Book 7 of The Asset-Based Mortgage Mastery Series, where we focus on one of the most powerful and underutilized segments of modern lending—foreign national asset-based mortgage loans.

For decades, the U.S. real estate market has been one of the most attractive investment environments in the world. Stability, legal protections, appreciation potential, rental income opportunities, and access to financing have made it a magnet for international investors. Yet, despite this demand, traditional mortgage systems have historically created barriers for foreign nationals. Many lenders rely heavily on U.S.-based income, U.S. credit history, and domestic financial documentation—requirements that immediately exclude highly qualified global buyers who possess significant assets but lack a U.S. financial footprint.

This is where asset-based mortgage lending transforms the game entirely. Instead of asking, "What is your income in the United States?" lenders begin asking a far more relevant question: "What assets do you control, and how can those assets support your ability to repay a loan?" This shift opens the door to a completely different type of borrower—one who may live in another country, earn income in foreign currencies, or operate businesses globally, yet still possesses substantial financial strength.

Foreign national asset-based mortgage loans are not simply an alternative product—they represent a new framework of thinking. They recognize that wealth is global, that liquidity exists in many forms, and that financial strength should not be judged solely by domestic documentation. In this book, you will learn how this framework works, how lenders evaluate global assets, and how borrowers can strategically position themselves to gain approval without traditional income verification.

One of the most important concepts to understand at the beginning of this journey is that international borrowers are not at a disadvantage—they are simply operating under a different set of rules. The key to success is not forcing yourself into the traditional U.S. mortgage box, but rather understanding how to navigate the system designed specifically for foreign nationals. This includes asset documentation, currency conversion, reserve requirements, risk mitigation, and lender overlays that are unique to this space.

Throughout this book, we will explore how global assets—such as international bank accounts, investment portfolios, business holdings, and even foreign real estate—can be used to qualify for mortgage financing in the United States. You will learn how lenders assess these assets, how they convert them into qualifying income equivalents, and how they determine overall borrower strength. More importantly, you will learn how to structure your financial profile in a way that aligns with lender expectations.

A major advantage of foreign national asset-based loans is flexibility. Unlike conventional loans, which often require strict documentation and rigid guidelines, asset-based programs are designed to accommodate complexity. This includes borrowers with multiple income streams, international business ownership, or non-traditional financial structures. The focus is not on fitting into a predefined box, but on demonstrating financial capacity through assets and reserves.

However, with this flexibility comes the need for precision. Foreign national loans involve additional layers of due diligence, including verification of foreign assets, translation of documents, compliance with international banking standards, and risk assessment related to currency fluctuations and geopolitical factors. Understanding these elements is essential, not only for approval but for long-term success as a borrower and investor.

This book is designed to give you a complete roadmap. Whether you are an international buyer looking to purchase a primary residence, a vacation home, or an investment property in the United States, or a mortgage professional seeking to expand your expertise in this high-demand niche, the strategies outlined here will provide clarity and direction. We will break down complex concepts into actionable steps, ensuring that you not only understand the process but can apply it effectively.

Another key theme you will encounter throughout this book is leverage. Asset-based lending allows borrowers to maintain control of their investments while still accessing capital. Instead of liquidating assets to purchase real estate, borrowers can use those assets as a foundation for financing. This preserves long-term growth potential while unlocking immediate opportunities in the U.S. market. For foreign nationals, this is especially powerful, as it allows them to diversify geographically without disrupting their existing financial strategies. We will also address common misconceptions that often discourage international buyers from pursuing U.S. real estate. Many believe that without a Social Security number, U.S. tax returns, or domestic credit history, financing is impossible. Others assume that cash purchases are the only option. In reality, asset-based mortgage programs are specifically designed to bridge these gaps, providing structured pathways to approval for borrowers who meet asset and reserve requirements.

As you move through this book, you will gain insight into how lenders view risk and how you can proactively address it. You will learn how to present your financial profile in a way that builds confidence, how to structure your assets for maximum impact, and how to navigate the approval process with clarity and control. This is not about guesswork—it is about strategy.

It is also important to recognize the broader opportunity that exists within foreign national lending. This is one of the fastest-growing segments of the mortgage industry, driven by increasing global wealth and demand for U.S. real estate. By understanding how to operate within this space, you position yourself at the intersection of global finance and domestic real estate—a powerful combination that offers long-term potential.

This book does not assume prior knowledge, but it does assume ambition. Whether you are starting from scratch or building on existing experience, the principles outlined here are designed to elevate your understanding and expand your capabilities. Each chapter will build upon the last, guiding you from foundational concepts to advanced strategies that can be applied in real-world scenarios.

By the end of this book, you will not only understand how foreign national asset-based mortgage loans work, but you will also be equipped to use them as a strategic tool. You will see beyond the limitations of traditional lending and recognize the possibilities that exist when assets become the primary driver of qualification.

The future of mortgage lending is not confined to local income or domestic borders. It is global, flexible, and asset-driven. This book is your guide to that future.

Chapter 1

Understanding Foreign National Asset-Based Mortgage Lending

Foreign national asset-based mortgage lending represents one of the most powerful evolutions in modern real estate finance, designed specifically for borrowers who do not reside in the United States but wish to purchase or refinance property within its borders. At its core, this lending approach shifts the focus away from traditional income verification and toward a borrower's asset strength, liquidity, and overall financial stability. For foreign nationals, this is not just a convenience—it is a necessity. Most international buyers do not have U.S.-based W-2 income, tax returns, or established credit profiles, yet many possess substantial wealth in the form of global assets. This chapter lays the foundation for understanding how lenders evaluate these borrowers and how asset-based lending bridges the gap between global wealth and U.S. real estate ownership.

To begin, it is important to define what constitutes a foreign national in the context of mortgage lending. A foreign national is typically an individual who resides outside the United States and does not have permanent residency or citizenship. This includes international investors, business owners, and high-net-worth individuals who may travel frequently or maintain financial ties across multiple countries. From a lender's perspective, these borrowers introduce additional layers of risk due to the absence of domestic financial records. However, rather than excluding them entirely, specialized loan programs have been developed to assess their financial strength through alternative methods.

The key differentiator in asset-based lending is the concept of asset depletion or asset utilization. Instead of analyzing income streams, lenders evaluate the borrower's total liquid and near-liquid assets and determine how those assets can support a mortgage payment over time. This includes cash in bank accounts, investment portfolios, retirement funds, and in some cases, even certain types of business assets. The lender then applies a structured formula to convert these assets into a theoretical income stream, which is used to qualify the borrower.

For foreign nationals, this process becomes even more nuanced due to the international nature of their assets. Funds may be held in foreign currencies, located in overseas financial institutions, or subject to different regulatory frameworks. Lenders must therefore account for currency conversion, transferability, and documentation standards when evaluating these assets. This is why foreign national asset-based loans often require a higher level of documentation compared to domestic asset-based loans, including translated bank statements, verification of account ownership, and proof of asset seasoning.

Another critical component of foreign national lending is the concept of reserves. Reserves refer to the amount of liquid assets a borrower has available after closing, typically expressed in months of mortgage payments. For foreign national loans, reserve requirements are often significantly higher than for traditional loans, sometimes ranging from 12 to 24 months or more. This serves as a risk mitigation tool for lenders, ensuring that the borrower has sufficient financial capacity to maintain payments even in the absence of verifiable income.

Loan-to-value ratios (LTV) also play a central role in foreign national asset-based lending. Because these loans involve additional risk factors, lenders typically require larger down payments, resulting in lower LTV ratios compared to conventional loans. While a domestic borrower might secure financing with as little as 5% down, a foreign national borrower may be required to invest 25% to 40% or more. This equity contribution not only reduces the lender's risk but also demonstrates the borrower's commitment to the transaction.

Credit evaluation is another area where foreign national loans differ significantly. In the absence of a U.S. credit score, lenders may rely on international credit reports, bank reference letters, or alternative credit documentation. In some cases, lenders may place greater emphasis on the borrower's asset profile rather than attempting to replicate a traditional credit analysis. This flexibility allows borrowers to qualify based on financial strength rather than conforming to rigid credit standards.

One of the most misunderstood aspects of foreign national lending is the role of income. While these loans are often described as "no income" or "no doc," this does not mean that the borrower's ability to repay is ignored. Instead, repayment capacity is assessed through assets rather than income streams. This distinction is crucial, as it highlights the fundamental shift in underwriting philosophy. The borrower is not exempt from demonstrating financial responsibility—they are simply doing so in a different way.

In addition to asset evaluation, lenders must also consider legal and regulatory factors. This includes compliance with anti-money laundering (AML) regulations, verification of the source of funds, and adherence to international banking standards. Borrowers may be required to provide detailed documentation regarding the origin of their assets, including business income, investment gains, or property sales. This ensures transparency and protects both the lender and the broader financial system. Another important consideration is property type and usage. Foreign national asset-based loans are commonly used for investment properties, vacation homes, or second residences, although some programs do allow for primary residence purchases. The intended use of the property can influence loan terms, including interest rates, reserve requirements, and documentation standards. Lenders may view investment properties as higher risk due to potential vacancy or market fluctuations, and this is reflected in the underwriting process.

Interest rates for foreign national loans are typically higher than those for conventional loans, reflecting the increased risk and complexity involved. However, for many borrowers, the ability to access financing without traditional income documentation outweighs the cost. Moreover, these loans provide an opportunity to leverage assets rather than liquidate them, preserving long-term investment growth while enabling immediate real estate acquisition.

As global wealth continues to expand, the demand for foreign national mortgage programs is expected to grow. International investors are increasingly seeking stable markets, and the United States remains a top destination due to its legal protections, economic strength, and diverse real estate opportunities. Asset-based lending plays a critical role in facilitating this demand, providing a pathway for qualified borrowers to participate in the market. Understanding the fundamentals of foreign national asset-based mortgage lending is the first step toward unlocking these opportunities. By recognizing how lenders evaluate assets, manage risk, and structure these loans, borrowers can position themselves strategically for approval. This chapter provides the foundation upon which the rest of the book will build, guiding you through more advanced strategies, documentation techniques, and real-world applications.

Ultimately, foreign national asset-based lending is not just about qualifying for a mortgage—it is about redefining what qualification means. It is about recognizing that financial strength is not limited to income statements or tax returns, but can be demonstrated through assets, liquidity, and strategic positioning. For international buyers, this represents a powerful shift, opening the door to opportunities that were once out of reach.

Real-Life Math Example: Applying Asset-Based Qualification for a Foreign National Borrower

To fully understand how foreign national asset-based mortgage lending works in practice, it is essential to walk through a detailed, real-life example that demonstrates how assets are converted into qualifying income and how a borrower meets lender requirements step by step. In this example, we will follow an international borrower who is purchasing a property in the United States using global assets rather than traditional income.

Consider a borrower named Daniel, a business owner based in Brazil. Daniel does not have U.S. income, a Social Security number, or a U.S. credit history. However, he has accumulated significant wealth through his business and investments. His financial profile includes $1,200,000 in a Brazilian bank account, $800,000 in a global investment portfolio, and an additional $200,000 in liquid reserves held in U.S. dollars. Daniel wants to purchase a property in Florida for $1,000,000 as an investment property.

The lender begins by evaluating Daniel's total qualifying assets. Not all assets are treated equally, and lenders often apply discounts or eligibility criteria depending on the asset type. In this case, the lender considers 100% of his liquid cash and 70% of his investment portfolio due to potential market volatility. This results in $1,200,000 from his bank account, $560,000 from his investments (70% of $800,000), and $200,000 in U.S. reserves, for a total of $1,960,000 in qualifying assets.

Next, the lender applies an asset depletion formula to convert these assets into a monthly income equivalent. A common approach is to divide the total qualifying assets by a fixed term, such as 60 months. In Daniel's case, $1,960,000 divided by 60 results in a theoretical monthly income of $32,666. This figure is then used to determine whether Daniel can support the mortgage payment.

Daniel plans to put 30% down on the $1,000,000 property, which equals $300,000. This leaves a loan amount of $700,000. Assuming an interest rate of 7.5% and a 30-year term, his estimated monthly principal and interest payment is approximately $4,900. When property taxes, insurance, and other costs are included, his total monthly housing expense is estimated at $6,200.

The lender then calculates Daniel's debt-to-income ratio using the asset-derived income. With a monthly income of $32,666 and a housing expense of $6,200, his ratio is approximately 19%, which is well within acceptable limits. This demonstrates that Daniel has more than sufficient financial capacity to support the loan.

In addition to income qualification, the lender evaluates Daniel's reserves. If the lender requires 12 months of reserves, Daniel must demonstrate access to at least $74,400 (12 months of $6,200 payments) after closing. Given his remaining assets, he easily meets this requirement.

Currency conversion is also considered in this process. Daniel's Brazilian assets are converted into U.S. dollars using current exchange rates, and the lender may apply a conservative adjustment to account for potential fluctuations. Documentation is translated and verified to ensure accuracy and compliance with lending standards.

Through this example, we see how a borrower with no U.S. income can successfully qualify for a mortgage using global assets. The process is systematic, transparent, and based on financial strength rather than traditional documentation. By understanding each step, borrowers can better prepare their financial profiles and approach the lending process with confidence.

This example illustrates the power of asset-based lending for foreign nationals. It transforms complex global financial situations into clear, quantifiable metrics that lenders can use to make informed decisions. For borrowers like Daniel, it opens the door to U.S. real estate ownership without requiring them to restructure their entire financial lives.

As you continue through this book, you will build upon this foundation, exploring more advanced scenarios, strategies, and optimization techniques. The goal is not only to understand the math, but to master the system behind it.

Chapter 2

Structuring and Documenting Global Assets for Mortgage Approval

One of the most critical factors in successfully obtaining a foreign national asset-based mortgage loan is not simply having assets, but knowing how to structure, document, and present those assets in a way that aligns with lender expectations. Many international borrowers possess substantial wealth, yet fail to qualify because their assets are not properly organized, verified, or positioned within the framework that lenders require. In this chapter, we will explore how to transform global assets into a clear, credible, and lender-ready financial profile that maximizes approval potential.

The first principle to understand is that lenders prioritize liquidity, stability, and verifiability. While a borrower may have millions in net worth, not all assets carry the same weight in the underwriting process. Liquid assets such as cash, publicly traded stocks, and readily accessible funds are considered the strongest because they can be quickly converted into usable capital. On the other hand, illiquid assets such as real estate holdings, private business equity, or collectibles may be recognized but often receive reduced value or are excluded entirely unless they can be clearly monetized.

For foreign nationals, liquidity takes on an even greater level of importance because lenders must evaluate not only the asset itself but also its accessibility across international borders. An asset that is technically valuable but difficult to transfer or convert into U.S. dollars may be discounted significantly. This is why borrowers are often advised to consolidate or reposition their assets prior to applying for a loan. Moving funds into internationally recognized financial institutions, converting holdings into more liquid forms, or organizing accounts under a clear ownership structure can dramatically improve the strength of an application.

Documentation is the next major pillar of the approval process. Lenders require detailed, verifiable records that demonstrate ownership, value, and history of the assets being used for qualification. This typically includes bank statements, brokerage account statements, letters from financial institutions, and in some cases, third-party verification reports. For foreign assets, these documents must often be translated into English and may need to meet specific formatting standards. Any inconsistencies, missing information, or unclear ownership structures can create delays or even result in denial.

One of the most overlooked aspects of documentation is asset seasoning. Seasoning refers to the length of time funds have been held in an account and can be verified through historical statements. Most lenders require at least two to three months of seasoning, although longer periods may be preferred for foreign national loans. This requirement is tied closely to compliance with anti-money laundering regulations, as lenders must ensure that funds are legitimate and not recently transferred for the sole purpose of qualifying for a loan. Borrowers who plan ahead and maintain consistent account histories are far more likely to navigate this requirement successfully.

Currency conversion is another essential component of structuring global assets. Because foreign nationals hold assets in various currencies, lenders must convert these values into U.S. dollars to determine qualification. However, this process is not always straightforward. Exchange rates fluctuate daily, and lenders may apply conservative adjustments to account for potential volatility. In some cases, a lender may use a slightly lower conversion rate than the current market rate to protect against currency risk. Borrowers should be aware of this and consider the impact of exchange rates on their qualifying asset totals.

In addition to conversion, lenders also evaluate the country of origin for the assets. Financial institutions in certain countries are considered more stable and transparent, while others may require additional scrutiny. Assets held in globally recognized banks or investment firms tend to carry more weight, as they are easier to verify and are perceived as lower risk. Borrowers with assets in less recognized institutions may need to provide additional documentation or transfer funds to more widely accepted accounts prior to applying.

Ownership structure plays a significant role in asset qualification as well. Lenders need to confirm that the borrower has full access and control over the assets being used. This can become complex when assets are held jointly, within business entities, or under trust structures. In such cases, additional documentation is required to demonstrate the borrower's authority to use those funds. For example, if assets are held within a corporation, the lender may require corporate documents, ownership percentages, and authorization letters confirming that the borrower can access those funds for personal use.

Another strategic consideration is the diversification of assets. While having a large concentration of wealth in a single account may appear strong, lenders often view diversified portfolios more favorably. A combination of cash reserves, investment accounts, and other liquid assets demonstrates financial stability and reduces perceived risk. It also provides flexibility in meeting various underwriting requirements, such as reserves, down payment funds, and asset depletion calculations.

Borrowers must also be mindful of the timing of asset transfers. Large, unexplained deposits can raise red flags during the underwriting process. Lenders will typically request explanations and supporting documentation for any significant changes in account balances. To avoid complications, borrowers should plan their financial movements well in advance and maintain clear records of all transactions. Transparency is key, and any attempt to obscure or simplify financial activity can lead to increased scrutiny.

In some cases, borrowers may choose to work with financial advisors or mortgage professionals who specialize in foreign national lending. These experts can provide guidance on how to structure assets effectively, identify potential issues before they arise, and ensure that documentation meets lender standards. While this may involve additional effort upfront, it can significantly streamline the approval process and increase the likelihood of success.

Another important factor is the alignment between the borrower's asset profile and the loan structure. Not all asset-based loan programs are the same, and different lenders may have varying requirements and guidelines. Understanding these differences allows borrowers to select the most appropriate program for their specific situation. For example, some lenders may place greater emphasis on liquid assets, while others may be more flexible in accepting certain types of investments. Matching the right borrower profile with the right lender is a critical step in the process.

As global financial systems continue to evolve, the ability to structure and document assets effectively will become an increasingly valuable skill. Foreign national borrowers who understand this process are not only more likely to secure financing, but also better positioned to leverage their assets strategically for future opportunities. This chapter serves as a roadmap for navigating these complexities, providing the tools and insights needed to present a strong and credible financial profile.

Ultimately, structuring and documenting global assets is about more than compliance—it is about strategy. It is about understanding how lenders think, anticipating their requirements, and positioning your financial profile in a way that aligns with their expectations. By mastering this process, you transform your assets from passive holdings into active tools for achieving real estate ownership in the United States.

Real-Life Math Example: Structuring and Qualifying Global Assets for Approval

To bring these concepts to life, let us walk through a detailed example of a foreign national borrower who must strategically restructure and document their assets in order to qualify for a U.S. mortgage. This example will highlight how asset organization, documentation, and conversion directly impact the borrower's ability to meet lender requirements.

Consider a borrower named Sofia, an entrepreneur based in Spain. Sofia has built a successful online business and accumulated wealth across multiple accounts. Her financial profile includes €900,000 in a European bank account, €600,000 in a diversified investment portfolio, and €300,000 held within a business account. She wishes to purchase a $1,200,000 property in Miami as a vacation home and rental investment.

At first glance, Sofia appears highly qualified. However, her assets are spread across different institutions, currencies, and ownership structures. The lender must evaluate which assets can be used, how they are converted, and whether they meet documentation standards.

The first step is currency conversion. Assuming an exchange rate of 1 euro to 1.10 U.S. dollars, Sofia's €900,000 bank account converts to $990,000. Her €600,000 investment portfolio converts to $660,000, and her €300,000 business account converts to $330,000. This results in a total of $1,980,000 in gross assets.

Next, the lender applies eligibility adjustments. Liquid personal funds are typically counted at 100%, while investment accounts may be discounted to 70%, and business funds may require additional verification or be discounted further. In Sofia's case, the lender counts $990,000 from her bank account, $462,000 from her investment portfolio (70% of $660,000), and $165,000 from her business account (50% of $330,000 due to access limitations). This results in $1,617,000 in qualifying assets.

Sofia plans to make a 35% down payment on the $1,200,000 property, which equals $420,000. This leaves a loan amount of $780,000. After subtracting the down payment from her qualifying assets, Sofia has $1,197,000 remaining.

The lender then applies an asset depletion formula, dividing the remaining assets by 60 months. This results in a monthly qualifying income of approximately $19,950. Sofia's estimated monthly housing expense, including principal, interest, taxes, and insurance, is $6,800. By comparing her asset-derived income to her housing expense, the lender calculates a ratio of approximately 34%, which falls within acceptable guidelines. Additionally, the lender requires 12 months of reserves, equal to $81,600. Sofia easily meets this requirement with her remaining assets.

However, before final approval, Sofia must address documentation and structuring issues. Her business account requires proof of ownership and authorization to use funds for personal purposes. Her investment portfolio statements must be translated into English, and her bank statements must show consistent balances over the past three months to meet seasoning requirements.

Sofia also chooses to consolidate a portion of her funds into a single internationally recognized bank to simplify verification and strengthen her application. This strategic move reduces complexity and increases lender confidence.

Through this example, we see how asset structuring directly impacts qualification. Without proper organization and documentation, Sofia's assets may have been discounted further or deemed insufficient. By understanding lender requirements and proactively aligning her financial profile, she successfully secures approval.

This example demonstrates that qualification is not just about how much you have, but how well your assets are presented. Strategic structuring, accurate documentation, and careful planning can significantly enhance a borrower's ability to access financing. As you continue through this book, you will learn how to refine these strategies and apply them to increasingly complex scenarios, ultimately mastering the art of asset-based mortgage qualification.

Chapter 3

Risk Assessment, Lender Overlays, and Strategic Positioning for Approval

As foreign national asset-based mortgage lending continues to grow, lenders have developed highly specialized methods to assess risk beyond the traditional frameworks used for domestic borrowers. While asset-based qualification opens the door for international buyers, approval is not automatic. Every loan must pass through a structured risk evaluation process that considers multiple layers of uncertainty, including borrower profile, asset stability, currency exposure, documentation reliability, and property characteristics. Understanding how lenders think about risk—and how to position yourself within that framework—is one of the most powerful advantages a borrower can have.

At the core of every lending decision is risk management. For foreign national borrowers, lenders face additional uncertainties compared to domestic loans. These include the borrower's distance from the property, lack of U.S. legal ties, limited or non-existent domestic credit history, and reliance on foreign financial systems. To offset these risks, lenders apply stricter guidelines, commonly referred to as overlays. These overlays are additional requirements layered on top of standard underwriting criteria, designed specifically to reduce exposure and protect the lender's investment.

One of the most important overlays is the loan-to-value ratio. As discussed previously, foreign national loans typically require larger down payments, but this is not just a general rule—it is a direct reflection of risk tolerance. A borrower with stronger assets, more stable documentation, and lower perceived risk may qualify for a higher loan-to-value ratio, while a borrower with more complex financials may be required to contribute additional equity. This dynamic creates an opportunity for strategic positioning, where borrowers can improve their profile to access better terms.

Another critical overlay is reserve requirements. For foreign national loans, reserves are not just a safety net—they are a primary indicator of borrower strength. Lenders often require 12 to 24 months of reserves, and in some cases even more. These reserves must typically be held in liquid or near-liquid form and must be verifiable. The presence of strong reserves can offset other perceived weaknesses, such as limited credit history or higher loan amounts. In many cases, increasing reserves is one of the fastest ways to strengthen an application.

Credit evaluation, while flexible, is still an important component of risk assessment. In the absence of a U.S. credit score, lenders rely on alternative methods such as international credit reports, bank reference letters, or documented payment histories. However, these substitutes are not always equivalent in the eyes of the lender. As a result, borrowers with limited credit documentation may face stricter overlays in other areas, such as lower loan-to-value ratios or higher reserve requirements. This interconnected nature of underwriting means that strengthening one area can often compensate for weaknesses in another.

Currency risk is another unique factor in foreign national lending. Because many borrowers hold assets in foreign currencies, lenders must consider the potential impact of exchange rate fluctuations on the borrower's financial stability. A borrower whose assets are denominated in a volatile currency may be viewed as higher risk, particularly if a significant depreciation could reduce their effective purchasing power. To mitigate this, lenders may apply conservative conversion rates or require additional reserves to account for potential fluctuations.

Documentation reliability is also a major consideration. Lenders must be confident that the information provided is accurate, verifiable, and consistent. This is particularly important when dealing with foreign financial institutions, where documentation standards may differ from those in the

United States. Inconsistencies, incomplete records, or unclear ownership structures can significantly increase perceived risk and may trigger additional scrutiny or even denial. Borrowers who present clear, well-organized, and professionally translated documentation are far more likely to gain lender confidence.

Property risk is another layer that must be considered. The type, location, and intended use of the property all influence the lender's risk assessment. Investment properties, for example, are generally considered higher risk than primary residences due to potential vacancy or market fluctuations. Similarly, properties in less stable or less liquid markets may be subject to stricter underwriting standards. Lenders evaluate not only the borrower's ability to repay, but also the underlying asset securing the loan.

Given these multiple layers of risk, strategic positioning becomes essential. Borrowers who understand how lenders evaluate risk can take proactive steps to strengthen their applications. This may include increasing the down payment, consolidating assets into more liquid forms, improving documentation quality, or selecting properties that align with lender preferences. Each of these actions reduces perceived risk and improves the likelihood of approval. One of the most effective strategies is to create redundancy in financial strength. Rather than relying on a single asset or account, borrowers can present multiple sources of liquidity and reserves. This demonstrates stability and reduces dependence on any one component of the financial profile. For example, a borrower with both cash reserves and investment accounts is viewed more favorably than one who relies solely on a single account, even if the total value is similar.

Another important strategy is timing. The way assets are positioned at the time of application can significantly impact the outcome. Borrowers who plan ahead—ensuring proper seasoning, stable balances, and clear documentation—are far more likely to navigate the underwriting process smoothly. Conversely, last-minute changes or unexplained transactions can create uncertainty and delay approval.

Working with the right lender is also a critical factor. Not all lenders have the same risk tolerance or expertise in foreign national lending. Some may specialize in high-net-worth borrowers and offer more flexible terms, while others may have stricter overlays and limited program options. Matching your financial profile with a lender that understands and accommodates your situation can make a significant difference in both approval and loan terms. It is also important to understand that risk assessment is not static. It is a dynamic process where multiple factors interact. A strong asset profile can offset weaker credit documentation, while a lower loan-to-value ratio can compensate for currency risk. This flexibility is one of the key advantages of asset-based lending, but it requires a strategic approach to fully leverage.

As you move forward, it is essential to view your financial profile through the lens of the lender. Every decision, from how assets are structured to how documentation is presented, should be aligned with reducing perceived risk. By doing so, you not only increase your chances of approval but also position yourself for more favorable loan terms.

Ultimately, risk is not something to be avoided–it is something to be managed. Foreign national asset-based mortgage lending provides a framework for managing that risk in a way that is both structured and flexible. By understanding the underlying principles and applying strategic positioning, borrowers can transform potential obstacles into opportunities.

Real-Life Math Example: Risk-Based Structuring and Approval Optimization

To illustrate how risk assessment and lender overlays impact real-world scenarios, let us examine a detailed example of a foreign national borrower navigating the approval process through strategic positioning. This example will demonstrate how adjustments in assets, reserves, and loan structure can significantly influence the outcome.

Consider a borrower named Ahmed, a real estate investor based in the United Arab Emirates. Ahmed has $2,500,000 in global assets, including $1,000,000 in cash, $1,000,000 in investment accounts, and $500,000 in business-related funds. He is interested in purchasing a $1,500,000 investment property in California.

Initially, Ahmed plans to put down 25%, or $375,000, resulting in a loan amount of $1,125,000. His remaining assets after the down payment total $2,125,000. The lender begins by applying eligibility adjustments, counting 100% of his cash, 70% of his investments ($700,000), and 50% of his business funds ($250,000), resulting in $1,950,000 in qualifying assets.

Using an asset depletion formula over 60 months, Ahmed's qualifying monthly income is calculated at $32,500. His estimated monthly housing expense is $9,500, resulting in a ratio of approximately 29%, which appears acceptable at first glance.

However, the lender identifies several risk factors. First, the 75% loan-to-value ratio is on the higher end for a foreign national investment property. Second, a portion of Ahmed's assets is held in a currency that has shown volatility. Third, his business funds require additional documentation to confirm accessibility.

To address these risks, the lender applies overlays, requiring either additional reserves or a lower loan-to-value ratio. Ahmed is presented with two options: increase his down payment to 35% or maintain the current structure but provide 18 months of reserves instead of 12.

Ahmed decides to increase his down payment to 35%, or $525,000, reducing the loan amount to $975,000. This adjustment lowers the lender's risk exposure and improves the overall profile. After the down payment, his remaining assets total $1,975,000, with $1,800,000 in qualifying assets after adjustments.

Recalculating the asset depletion, $1,800,000 divided by 60 results in a monthly income of $30,000. His new housing expense is approximately $8,200, resulting in a ratio of 27%, which is even stronger than before.

Additionally, the lower loan-to-value ratio reduces the lender's concern about property risk and market fluctuations. Ahmed also provides additional documentation for his business funds and converts a portion of his assets into U.S. dollars to mitigate currency risk. Through these strategic adjustments,

Ahmed transforms a borderline approval scenario into a strong, low-risk application. Not only does he secure the loan, but he also qualifies for slightly better terms due to the improved risk profile.

This example highlights the importance of understanding how different variables interact within the underwriting process. Small changes in down payment, asset allocation, or documentation can have a significant impact on the final outcome. By approaching the process strategically, borrowers can actively shape their approval rather than passively waiting for a decision.

As you continue through this book, you will learn how to apply these principles to increasingly complex scenarios, allowing you to navigate the foreign national lending landscape with confidence and precision.

Chapter 4

Loan Programs, Terms, and Structuring Options for Foreign National Borrowers

As foreign national asset-based mortgage lending continues to expand, a wide variety of loan programs and structuring options have emerged to accommodate different borrower profiles, property types, and investment goals. Understanding these programs is essential because not all loans are created equal, and the structure you choose can significantly impact your approval, cash flow, long-term returns, and overall financial flexibility. In this chapter, we will break down the most common loan types available to foreign national borrowers, explore how terms are structured, and explain how to align the right program with your specific strategy.

The first major distinction to understand is between fixed-rate and adjustable-rate mortgage structures. Fixed-rate loans provide stability by locking in the interest rate for the life of the loan, typically 30 years. This is particularly attractive for foreign national borrowers who want predictable payments and long-term security, especially when investing in rental properties. On the other hand, adjustable-rate mortgages (ARMs) offer lower initial interest rates for a fixed period—such as 5, 7, or 10 years—after which the rate adjusts periodically based on market conditions. For investors who plan to sell or refinance within a shorter timeframe, ARMs can provide significant cost savings during the initial period.

Another key component of loan structuring is the term length. While 30-year amortization is the most common, some foreign national programs offer 25-year or even 20-year terms. Shorter terms result in higher monthly payments but reduce total interest paid over time and build equity more quickly. Borrowers must balance affordability with long-term financial goals when selecting the appropriate term.

Interest-only options are another powerful tool available in many foreign national loan programs. With an interest-only loan, the borrower pays only the interest for a specified period, typically 5 to 10 years, before transitioning to full amortization. This structure significantly reduces the initial monthly payment, improving cash flow and making it easier to qualify. For investors, this can be particularly advantageous when managing multiple properties or maximizing rental income. However, it is important to understand that the principal balance does not decrease during the interest-only period, which can impact long-term equity growth.

Loan-to-value ratios vary widely depending on the program, borrower profile, and property type. While some lenders may offer up to 75% LTV for strong borrowers, others may cap at 60% to 70% depending on risk factors. Higher loan amounts, luxury properties, or less liquid asset profiles may require lower LTVs. Understanding where you fall within this spectrum allows you to plan your capital allocation more effectively and avoid surprises during the approval process.

Property type plays a significant role in determining loan structure. Investment properties, second homes, and primary residences are all evaluated differently. Investment properties typically carry higher interest rates and stricter requirements due to perceived risk, while second homes may offer slightly more favorable terms. Some lenders restrict foreign national borrowers to non-owner-occupied properties, while others allow for more flexibility. Matching your intended use with the right program is critical for both approval and long-term success.

Another important factor is prepayment penalties. Many foreign national loans include prepayment penalties, which are fees charged if the borrower pays off the loan early within a specified period. These penalties are often structured as a percentage of the remaining balance and may decline over time. While this can be a drawback for borrowers seeking flexibility, it often allows lenders to offer more competitive interest rates. Understanding how prepayment penalties work—and whether they align with your investment timeline—is essential when selecting a loan program.

Documentation requirements also vary by program. Some lenders offer streamlined asset-based loans with minimal documentation, while others require more detailed verification, especially for higher loan amounts. Borrowers with well-organized and easily verifiable assets may benefit from simpler programs, while those with more complex financial profiles may need to work within more structured guidelines. Choosing the right program based on your documentation readiness can significantly impact both speed and outcome.

Geographic considerations also influence loan availability and terms. Certain lenders specialize in specific markets, such as major metropolitan areas or high-demand investment regions. Properties located in these areas may benefit from more favorable terms due to stronger market stability and liquidity. Conversely, properties in less established markets may face stricter guidelines or limited program availability. Understanding these geographic nuances allows borrowers to align their investment strategy with lender preferences.

Another advanced structuring option involves cross-collateralization, where a borrower uses multiple properties or asset pools to secure a single loan. While less common, this approach can increase borrowing capacity and provide additional flexibility for high-net-worth borrowers. However, it also introduces additional complexity and risk, as multiple assets are tied to a single obligation. This strategy is typically best suited for experienced investors with a clear understanding of its implications.

Currency considerations also extend into loan structuring. While most foreign national loans are denominated in U.S. dollars, borrowers may need to consider how currency fluctuations impact their ability to make payments. Some borrowers choose to maintain dollar-denominated accounts or hedge currency exposure to reduce risk. This becomes particularly important for long-term loans where exchange rate volatility can have a significant cumulative effect.

One of the most powerful aspects of loan structuring is the ability to align financing with investment strategy. For example, a borrower focused on long-term appreciation may prioritize a fixed-rate loan with no prepayment penalty, while a short-term investor may choose an ARM with lower initial payments and a defined exit strategy. Similarly, a borrower seeking maximum cash flow may opt for an interest-only structure, while one focused on equity growth may prefer full amortization. Selecting the right loan program is not just about approval—it is about optimization. It is about choosing a structure that supports your financial goals, minimizes risk, and maximizes opportunity. This requires a deep understanding of available options, as well as a clear vision of your investment strategy.

As you move forward, it is essential to approach loan structuring with intention. Every decision, from interest rate type to term length, should be aligned with your broader financial objectives. By doing so, you transform your mortgage from a simple financing tool into a strategic asset that supports long-term growth.

Real-Life Math Example: Comparing Loan Structures and Their Impact on Cash Flow and Qualification

To fully understand how different loan structures impact both qualification and long-term performance, let us examine a detailed example of a foreign national borrower evaluating multiple financing options for the same property.

Consider a borrower named Li Wei, an investor from China with $2,000,000 in liquid and semi-liquid assets. Li Wei is purchasing a $1,200,000 rental property in Los Angeles and plans to put down 30%, or $360,000. This results in a loan amount of $840,000. After applying asset eligibility adjustments, Li Wei has $1,400,000 in qualifying assets remaining. The lender calculates his asset-based income by dividing $1,400,000 by 60 months, resulting in $23,333 per month. The lender then evaluates three different loan structures to determine both qualification and strategic fit.

In the first scenario, Li Wei chooses a 30-year fixed-rate mortgage at 7.25%. The monthly principal and interest payment is approximately $5,730. Including taxes and insurance, the total monthly housing expense is $7,200. This results in a ratio of approximately 31%, which is within acceptable limits.

In the second scenario, Li Wei selects a 7-year ARM with an initial rate of 6.5%. The monthly principal and interest payment drops to approximately $5,310, with a total housing expense of $6,800. This lowers the ratio to approximately 29%, improving qualification and increasing monthly cash flow.

In the third scenario, Li Wei chooses an interest-only loan at 6.75% for the first 10 years. The monthly interest-only payment is approximately $4,725, with a total housing expense of $6,200. This results in a ratio of approximately 26%, providing the strongest qualification profile and the highest cash flow.

From a qualification standpoint, all three options are viable.

However, the differences in monthly payment and long-term implications are significant. The interest-only option provides the lowest payment and highest cash flow, making it ideal for maximizing rental income. The ARM offers a balance between lower initial cost and gradual equity growth. The fixed-rate option provides long-term stability and predictable payments.

Li Wei must also consider reserves. Assuming a requirement of 12 months of reserves, the required amount varies based on the monthly payment. For the fixed-rate loan, reserves must cover $86,400, while the interest-only option requires only $74,400. This difference further impacts overall liquidity and flexibility.

Additionally, Li Wei evaluates prepayment penalties. The ARM and interest-only options include a three-year prepayment penalty, while the fixed-rate loan does not. If Li Wei plans to sell or refinance within that period, this cost must be factored into the decision.

By comparing these scenarios, Li Wei gains a clear understanding of how loan structure impacts both qualification and strategy. Rather than simply choosing the first available option, he selects the interest-only loan to maximize cash flow while maintaining flexibility for future investments.

This example demonstrates that loan structuring is not just a technical decision—it is a strategic one. By analyzing the numbers and aligning them with investment goals, borrowers can optimize their financing and create a more efficient and effective real estate portfolio. As you continue through this book, you will learn how to refine these strategies, adapt them to different market conditions, and apply them to increasingly complex scenarios. The goal is not just to qualify, but to structure your financing in a way that supports long-term success.

Chapter 5

Navigating the Loan Process, Timelines, and Closing Strategies for Foreign National Borrowers

Securing a foreign national asset-based mortgage loan is not just about qualifying on paper—it is about successfully navigating a multi-step process that involves coordination, timing, documentation, and strategic execution. While the fundamentals of underwriting and asset qualification form the backbone of approval, the actual loan process introduces a new layer of complexity that can determine whether a transaction moves forward smoothly or becomes delayed, renegotiated, or even canceled. In this chapter, we will walk through the full lifecycle of a foreign national loan, from pre-qualification to closing, and explore how borrowers can position themselves for efficiency, certainty, and success.

The process begins with pre-qualification, which is often the most underestimated stage. For foreign national borrowers, pre-qualification is not simply a preliminary estimate—it is a critical step that establishes credibility with sellers, agents, and lenders. During this phase, the borrower provides an overview of their assets, intended property type, and investment goals.

A knowledgeable lender or broker will evaluate this information and provide a preliminary assessment of eligibility, loan amount, and required documentation. This step allows borrowers to identify potential issues early and begin structuring their assets accordingly.

Once pre-qualified, the next step is property selection and contract execution. In competitive markets, foreign national borrowers may face additional challenges due to perceived uncertainty around financing. This is why a strong pre-qualification, often accompanied by a lender letter, is essential. It demonstrates that the borrower has already been evaluated and is capable of completing the transaction. In some cases, borrowers may also choose to provide proof of funds to further strengthen their position.

After the purchase contract is executed, the loan application moves into the formal underwriting phase. This is where the borrower submits detailed documentation, including asset statements, identification, and any required translations. For foreign national loans, this stage often involves more extensive verification than domestic loans. Lenders must confirm the authenticity of foreign financial documents, verify account ownership, and ensure compliance with regulatory requirements. Borrowers who have prepared their documentation in advance will experience a significantly smoother process.

The appraisal process runs concurrently with underwriting. The lender orders an independent appraisal to determine the value of the property and ensure it meets lending standards. For foreign national borrowers, appraisal requirements are generally similar to those for domestic loans, but timing can vary depending on location and property type. A low appraisal can impact the loan-to-value ratio and may require the borrower to increase their down payment or renegotiate the purchase price.

Another critical component of the process is the verification of funds. Lenders must ensure that the funds used for the down payment and closing costs are legitimate, seasoned, and transferable. This often involves tracing the origin of funds, reviewing transaction histories, and confirming that funds can be moved into the United States. International wire transfers, currency conversion, and banking regulations can all affect this stage, making early planning essential.

As underwriting progresses, the lender may issue conditions—specific requirements that must be satisfied before final approval. These conditions can range from additional documentation requests to clarifications of existing information. For foreign national borrowers, common conditions include updated asset statements, proof of asset transferability, and verification of business ownership. Responding to these conditions quickly and accurately is key to maintaining momentum and avoiding delays.

One of the most important aspects of the loan process is timeline management. Foreign national loans typically take longer to close than domestic loans, often ranging from 30 to 60 days or more. This extended timeline is due to the additional layers of verification and documentation involved. Borrowers must account for this when negotiating contract terms and ensure that closing deadlines are realistic. Working with experienced professionals who understand these timelines can make a significant difference.

Closing preparation is another stage where strategic planning is essential. Borrowers must ensure that all funds are available in the correct accounts, that wire instructions are confirmed, and that any required signatures or notarizations are completed. For international borrowers, this may involve coordinating with overseas banks, scheduling remote notarizations, or working with U.S.-based representatives. Any delays at this stage can jeopardize the transaction, making preparation critical.

The closing itself involves the final execution of loan documents, transfer of funds, and recording of the property. Depending on the borrower's location, this may be completed in person or through remote closing procedures. Once the transaction is finalized, the borrower becomes the official owner of the property, and the loan enters the servicing phase.

Post-closing considerations are equally important. Borrowers must ensure that mortgage payments are set up correctly, that property management arrangements are in place if the property is an investment, and that any currency or banking strategies are aligned with ongoing payment obligations. Maintaining a stable financial profile after closing is also important for future refinancing or additional purchases.

One of the most effective ways to navigate the loan process is through proactive communication. Borrowers who stay engaged, respond quickly to requests, and maintain transparency throughout the process are far more likely to achieve successful outcomes. This includes regular communication with lenders, agents, and any other parties involved in the transaction.

Another key strategy is building a strong team. Working with experienced mortgage professionals, real estate agents, and legal advisors who specialize in foreign national transactions can significantly reduce complexity and risk. These professionals understand the nuances of the process and can provide guidance at each stage, ensuring that potential issues are addressed before they become obstacles.

Ultimately, the loan process is where strategy meets execution. All of the preparation, structuring, and positioning discussed in previous chapters culminate in this stage. By understanding each step, anticipating challenges, and approaching the process with a clear plan, borrowers can navigate even the most complex transactions with confidence.

Real-Life Math Example: Timeline, Cash Flow Planning, and Closing Execution

To illustrate how the loan process unfolds in real life, let us examine a detailed example of a foreign national borrower managing both financial calculations and timeline execution throughout a transaction.

Consider a borrower named Carlos, an investor from Mexico with $1,800,000 in qualifying assets. Carlos is purchasing a $900,000 rental property in Orlando and plans to put down 30%, or $270,000. This results in a loan amount of $630,000. After applying asset eligibility adjustments, Carlos has $1,300,000 in qualifying assets remaining.

The lender calculates Carlos's asset-based income by dividing $1,300,000 by 60 months, resulting in $21,666 per month. His estimated monthly housing expense, including principal, interest, taxes, and insurance, is $5,800, resulting in a ratio of approximately 27%, which meets underwriting guidelines.

Carlos enters into a purchase contract with a 45-day closing timeline. During the first 10 days, he submits all required documentation, including translated bank statements and proof of asset ownership. The appraisal is ordered and completed within 15 days, confirming the property value at $900,000.

At day 20, the lender issues conditional approval, requesting updated asset statements and verification of funds for closing. Carlos transfers $300,000 into a U.S. account to cover the down payment and closing costs, ensuring that funds are readily accessible. This transfer takes 5 business days due to international banking processes.

By day 30, Carlos satisfies all conditions, and the loan moves to final approval. The lender confirms that Carlos meets the reserve requirement of 12 months, which equals $69,600. With over $1,000,000 remaining in assets, he easily exceeds this requirement.

During the final 10 days, Carlos prepares for closing by

confirming wire instructions, coordinating with the title company, and ensuring that all documents are signed and notarized. On day 45, the transaction closes successfully, and Carlos becomes the owner of the property.

From a financial perspective, Carlos evaluates his cash flow. The property generates $6,500 per month in rental income, while his total monthly housing expense is $5,800, resulting in a positive cash flow of $700 per month. This aligns with his investment strategy and provides additional financial flexibility.

Carlos also considers future opportunities. With over $1,000,000 in remaining assets, he has the capacity to pursue additional investments. By maintaining strong reserves and a stable financial profile, he positions himself for future financing.

This example demonstrates how financial calculations and timeline management intersect in the loan process. Every step, from asset structuring to fund transfers, must be executed with precision to ensure a successful outcome. By planning ahead and understanding each phase, borrowers can navigate the process efficiently and achieve their investment goals.

As you continue through this book, you will build on these principles, learning how to streamline processes, optimize timelines, and execute transactions with confidence and control.

Chapter 6

Scaling a U.S. Real Estate Portfolio as a Foreign National Using Asset-Based Financing

Once a foreign national borrower successfully acquires their first property using an asset-based mortgage, the next strategic step is not simply ownership—it is expansion. The true power of asset-based lending lies in its ability to be repeated, scaled, and optimized over time. Unlike traditional lending, which is often constrained by income limits, asset-based financing allows borrowers to leverage their global wealth repeatedly, creating a pathway to build a diversified and income-producing real estate portfolio in the United States. This chapter focuses on how to transition from a single transaction to a scalable system that generates long-term growth, cash flow, and financial leverage.

The foundation of scaling begins with understanding leverage. Leverage is the ability to control a larger asset using a smaller amount of capital. In the context of real estate, this means using a down payment to acquire a property while the lender finances the majority of the purchase. For foreign national borrowers, asset-based lending allows this process to be repeated as long as sufficient assets and reserves remain available. The key is not to deploy all capital into one transaction, but to allocate it strategically across multiple acquisitions.

A common mistake among first-time international investors is over-concentration. They may invest a large portion of their assets into a single property, leaving limited liquidity for future opportunities. While this may result in ownership, it restricts scalability. A more effective approach is to preserve liquidity by maintaining a balance between down payments, reserves, and remaining investable assets. This ensures that each acquisition supports the next, creating a compounding effect over time.

Portfolio scaling also requires an understanding of lender exposure limits. Many lenders place caps on the number of properties or total loan amounts they are willing to extend to a single borrower. This is where working with multiple lenders becomes a strategic advantage. By diversifying lending relationships, borrowers can continue to expand their portfolio without being constrained by a single institution's limits. Each lender evaluates risk independently, allowing borrowers to structure multiple loans across different programs.

Another critical factor in scaling is property selection. Not all properties contribute equally to portfolio growth. Investors must evaluate potential acquisitions based on cash flow, appreciation potential, market stability, and ease of management. Properties that generate consistent rental income can help offset mortgage payments and improve overall portfolio performance. At the same time, properties in strong appreciation markets can build equity, which can later be leveraged for additional acquisitions.

Cash flow management becomes increasingly important as the portfolio grows. Each property introduces new expenses, including mortgage payments, property taxes, insurance, maintenance, and management fees. Investors must ensure that rental income or other financial resources are sufficient to cover these obligations. Positive cash flow not only supports the portfolio but also enhances the borrower's financial profile for future lending.

Asset recycling is another powerful concept in scaling. As properties appreciate in value or as loans are paid down, equity is created. This equity can be accessed through refinancing or other financial strategies, providing additional capital for new investments. For foreign national borrowers, asset-based refinancing programs offer a way to unlock this equity without relying on traditional income documentation.

This creates a cycle where assets generate equity, equity generates capital, and capital fuels further growth. Diversification is essential in managing risk within a growing portfolio. This includes diversifying across property types, geographic locations, and tenant profiles. By spreading investments across different markets and asset classes, borrowers can reduce exposure to localized economic downturns or market fluctuations. Diversification also enhances stability, making the portfolio more resilient over time.

Currency management continues to play a role in portfolio scaling. As borrowers acquire multiple properties in the United States, they must consider how exchange rate fluctuations impact both asset values and cash flow. Some investors choose to maintain U.S. dollar accounts or reinvest rental income within the U.S. to reduce currency exposure. This strategic alignment helps stabilize financial performance and simplifies ongoing operations.

Operational efficiency becomes increasingly important as the portfolio expands. Managing multiple properties from another country requires systems, processes, and reliable partners. Property management companies, accountants, and legal advisors play a critical role in ensuring that the portfolio operates smoothly. Investors who build strong operational infrastructure can scale more effectively and with less risk.

Another advanced strategy involves staggered acquisitions. Rather than purchasing multiple properties simultaneously, investors can space out acquisitions over time. This allows for better management of cash flow, reserves, and market conditions. It also provides opportunities to adjust strategy based on performance and evolving goals. Staggering acquisitions creates a more controlled and sustainable growth trajectory.

Risk management remains a central theme throughout the scaling process. As the portfolio grows, so does the potential impact of market changes, vacancies, or unexpected expenses. Maintaining strong reserves, monitoring market trends, and continuously evaluating performance are essential practices. Borrowers who approach scaling with discipline and strategy are far more likely to achieve long-term success.

One of the most powerful aspects of asset-based lending is its flexibility. Borrowers are not locked into a single path—they can adapt their strategy as their portfolio evolves. Whether focusing on cash flow, appreciation, or a combination of both, asset-based financing provides the tools needed to pursue a wide range of investment objectives.

Ultimately, scaling a real estate portfolio is not about acquiring as many properties as possible—it is about building a system that generates consistent returns, preserves capital, and creates opportunities for continued growth. By understanding leverage, managing risk, and aligning financing with strategy, foreign national borrowers can transform a single investment into a long-term wealth-building platform.

Real-Life Math Example: Scaling from One Property to a Multi-Property Portfolio

To illustrate how portfolio scaling works in practice, let us examine a detailed example of a foreign national borrower building a real estate portfolio using asset-based financing over multiple transactions.

Consider a borrower named Elena, an investor from Colombia with $2,500,000 in qualifying assets. Elena begins by purchasing her first property in Miami for $800,000. She puts down 30%, or $240,000, resulting in a loan amount of $560,000. After the purchase, she has $2,260,000 in remaining assets.

The lender calculates her asset-based income by dividing $2,260,000 by 60 months, resulting in $37,666 per month. Her monthly housing expense for the first property is $5,200, resulting in a ratio of approximately 14%, leaving significant capacity for additional investments.

The property generates $5,800 per month in rental income, creating a positive cash flow of $600. Elena decides to reinvest this income into her portfolio rather than withdrawing it, increasing her available capital over time.

Six months later, Elena identifies a second property priced at $700,000. She again puts down 30%, or $210,000, resulting in a loan amount of $490,000. Her remaining assets are now $2,050,000. After applying asset eligibility adjustments, she maintains strong qualifying income and meets all reserve requirements.

Her total monthly housing expenses across both properties are $9,800, while her combined rental income is $11,200, resulting in a net positive cash flow of $1,400 per month. This additional income strengthens her financial profile and supports further expansion.

One year later, Elena's first property has appreciated to $900,000, creating $100,000 in additional equity. She uses an asset-based refinancing program to access a portion of this equity, extracting $60,000 in cash. Combined with her existing assets, she uses this capital to fund the down payment for a third property priced at $750,000.

After acquiring the third property, Elena's total portfolio value reaches $2,350,000, with three income-producing assets. Her total monthly housing expenses are $14,500, while her combined rental income is $16,800, resulting in a net cash flow of $2,300 per month. At this stage, Elena still maintains over $1,500,000 in remaining assets, providing strong reserves and the ability to continue scaling. By carefully managing her down payments, leveraging appreciation, and reinvesting cash flow, she has built a multi-property portfolio without relying on traditional income.

This example demonstrates the compounding effect of asset-based lending. Each property contributes to the next, creating a cycle of growth that accelerates over time. By maintaining discipline, managing risk, and aligning financing with strategy, Elena transforms her initial investment into a scalable and sustainable portfolio.

As you move forward, consider how these principles apply to your own situation. Scaling is not a one-time event—it is an ongoing process that requires planning, execution, and adaptability. With the right approach, asset-based financing can serve as the foundation for long-term real estate success in the United States.

Chapter 7

Exit Strategies, Refinancing, and Long-Term Wealth Optimization for Foreign National Borrowers

As foreign national investors build portfolios using asset-based mortgage financing, the ultimate objective extends far beyond acquisition. True mastery lies in knowing how to exit, reposition, refinance, and optimize assets over time to maximize returns, preserve capital, and maintain flexibility in a constantly evolving global financial landscape. This chapter focuses on the strategies that allow borrowers not only to enter the U.S. real estate market, but to strategically manage and eventually exit or transform their investments for long-term wealth creation.

The first concept to understand is that every real estate investment should begin with an exit strategy in mind. Whether the goal is to sell, refinance, hold for long-term appreciation, or transition into a different asset class, having a clear plan from the beginning provides direction and discipline. For foreign national borrowers, exit strategies must also account for cross-border considerations, including currency exchange, taxation, and capital movement. One of the most common exit strategies is property appreciation and sale. As the U.S. real estate market grows, properties increase in value, allowing investors to realize gains upon sale. However, timing plays a critical role. Selling too early may limit potential appreciation, while holding too long may expose the investor to market downturns. Successful investors monitor market trends, economic indicators, and local conditions to identify optimal exit points.

Another powerful strategy is refinancing. Rather than selling a property, borrowers can refinance to access equity while retaining ownership. Asset-based refinancing programs allow foreign national borrowers to extract cash without traditional income verification, making this an attractive option for reinvestment. This strategy enables investors to recycle capital, fund new acquisitions, or improve liquidity without disrupting their portfolio.

Cash-out refinancing is particularly effective when combined with appreciation. As property values increase and loan balances decrease, equity grows. By refinancing at a higher property value, borrowers can convert this equity into usable capital. This process can be repeated over time, creating a cycle of growth where assets generate new opportunities.

Debt optimization is another key component of long-term strategy. Not all debt is equal, and the structure of a loan can significantly impact overall returns. Borrowers may choose to refinance into lower interest rates, switch from adjustable to fixed rates, or restructure loans to improve cash flow. These adjustments can enhance profitability and reduce risk over time.

Tax considerations are also critical for foreign national investors. U.S. real estate transactions are subject to various tax regulations, including withholding requirements and capital gains taxes. Understanding these rules—and working with experienced tax professionals—allows investors to structure transactions in a way that minimizes liabilities and maximizes net returns. This may involve holding properties through specific entities, timing sales strategically, or utilizing tax treaties between countries.

Currency strategy becomes increasingly important during exit and refinancing. Exchange rate fluctuations can significantly impact the value of returns when converting proceeds back into the investor's home currency. Some investors choose to time currency conversions strategically, while others maintain U.S. dollar holdings to reduce exposure. Aligning currency strategy with investment goals is essential for preserving gains.

Portfolio rebalancing is another advanced strategy used by experienced investors. Over time, certain properties may outperform others, or market conditions may shift. Rebalancing involves selling or refinancing underperforming assets and reallocating capital into higher-performing opportunities. This ensures that the portfolio remains aligned with the investor's objectives and adapts to changing conditions.

Another important consideration is liquidity planning. While real estate is a powerful wealth-building tool, it is inherently less liquid than other asset classes. Investors must ensure that they maintain sufficient liquid reserves to cover expenses, manage risks, and capitalize on new opportunities. Asset-based lending supports this by allowing borrowers to leverage assets without fully liquidating them.

Long-term wealth optimization also involves generational planning. Many foreign national investors view U.S. real estate as a legacy asset that can be passed down to future generations. Structuring ownership through trusts, corporations, or other entities can facilitate this process and provide additional legal and financial benefits. This forward-thinking approach transforms real estate from a short-term investment into a multi-generational wealth strategy.

Risk management remains a constant throughout the lifecycle of an investment. Market fluctuations, economic changes, and unforeseen events can impact property values and cash flow. Investors must continuously monitor performance, adjust strategies, and maintain reserves to navigate these challenges. A proactive approach to risk ensures stability and resilience over time.

One of the most powerful aspects of asset-based lending is its ability to support multiple exit and optimization strategies simultaneously. Borrowers are not locked into a single path—they can adapt, refinance, sell, or hold based on market conditions and personal goals. This flexibility is a key advantage in a dynamic global environment.

Ultimately, the goal of exit and optimization strategies is not simply to maximize profit, but to create a sustainable system of wealth generation. By understanding how to manage assets over time, foreign national borrowers can transform individual transactions into a cohesive, long-term strategy that supports financial independence and growth.

Real-Life Math Example: Refinancing, Equity Extraction, and Strategic Exit Planning

To illustrate how these strategies work in practice, let us examine a detailed example of a foreign national investor optimizing a portfolio through refinancing and strategic exits. Consider a borrower named Marco, an investor from Italy who has built a portfolio of three properties in the United States over five years. His initial total investment was $1,800,000 across three properties, with a combined loan balance of $1,200,000. Over time, the properties have appreciated, and the total portfolio value is now $2,400,000.

Marco's current equity in the portfolio is $1,200,000 ($2,400,000 value minus $1,200,000 loan balance). He decides to explore a cash-out refinancing strategy to access a portion of this equity for new investments.

The lender offers a refinance at 70% loan-to-value. Based on the new portfolio value of $2,400,000, the maximum loan amount is $1,680,000. After paying off the existing loan balance of $1,200,000, Marco can extract $480,000 in cash.

The new loan carries an interest rate of 6.75%, with a monthly payment of approximately $10,900. Previously, Marco's combined monthly payments were $8,500. While his payment increases, his portfolio now includes an additional $480,000 in liquidity.

Marco uses $300,000 of the extracted cash as a down payment on a fourth property valued at $1,000,000. The remaining $180,000 is held as reserves and for future opportunities. The new property generates $7,000 per month in rental income, while its monthly expense is $5,800, resulting in a positive cash flow of $1,200.

After the refinance and new acquisition, Marco's total portfolio value increases to $3,400,000, with a combined loan balance of $2,380,000. His total monthly housing expenses are $16,700, while his combined rental income is $20,500, resulting in a net cash flow of $3,800 per month.

Marco then evaluates his exit strategy for one of his original properties, which has appreciated significantly but generates lower cash flow compared to the others. He sells the property for $900,000, realizing a gain of $300,000. After taxes and expenses, he nets approximately $250,000, which he reinvests into higher-performing assets.

By combining refinancing, equity extraction, and strategic sales, Marco transforms his portfolio into a more efficient and higher-performing system. His assets continue to generate income, his equity is actively deployed, and his overall wealth continues to grow.

This example demonstrates the power of long-term strategy in asset-based lending. It is not just about acquiring properties—it is about managing them intelligently, leveraging equity, and adapting to changing conditions. By mastering these concepts, foreign national borrowers can achieve a level of financial control and growth that extends far beyond a single transaction.

As you complete this book, you now have a comprehensive framework for entering, navigating, scaling, and optimizing the U.S. real estate market using asset-based mortgage strategies. The next step is execution—applying these principles with clarity, discipline, and confidence to achieve your financial goals.

Chapter 8

Advanced Portfolio Optimization, Global Structuring, and Legacy Wealth Strategies for Foreign National Investors

As foreign national investors progress from acquisition and scaling into a more mature stage of portfolio ownership, the focus naturally shifts toward optimization, protection, and long-term wealth preservation. At this level, success is no longer defined solely by the number of properties owned or even total portfolio value, but by efficiency, structure, control, and the ability to sustain and transfer wealth across generations. Asset-based mortgage lending continues to play a central role in this evolution, providing the flexibility and leverage needed to refine and expand a global real estate strategy.

One of the most important concepts at this stage is portfolio efficiency. Efficiency refers to how well your assets are performing relative to the capital deployed. This includes evaluating return on equity, cash flow yield, appreciation potential, and overall risk exposure. As properties appreciate and loans amortize, equity builds—but idle equity does not generate income. Advanced investors continuously evaluate whether their equity is being used effectively or whether it can be repositioned into higher-performing opportunities.

This leads to the concept of equity optimization. Rather than allowing equity to remain trapped within properties, investors can strategically access and redeploy it through refinancing or restructuring. Asset-based refinance programs make this possible without the need for traditional income documentation, allowing foreign national borrowers to unlock capital while maintaining ownership. The key is to balance leverage with stability, ensuring that increased borrowing does not compromise long-term sustainability.

Global structuring becomes increasingly important as portfolios grow. Many foreign national investors hold assets across multiple countries, currencies, and legal systems. Structuring ownership through appropriate entities—such as limited liability companies, holding companies, or international trusts—can provide benefits related to liability protection, tax efficiency, and estate planning. While the specifics vary based on jurisdiction, the underlying principle is to create a structure that aligns with both investment goals and legal requirements.

Tax efficiency is a critical component of advanced portfolio management. U.S. real estate investments are subject to federal, state, and sometimes local taxes, and foreign nationals must also consider tax implications in their home countries. Strategic planning can significantly reduce tax burdens, whether through entity structuring, timing of transactions, or leveraging applicable treaties. Working with experienced tax advisors is essential at this stage, as even small adjustments can have a significant impact on net returns.

Another key strategy is income layering. Rather than relying solely on rental income, advanced investors often create multiple streams of income within their portfolio. This can include short-term rentals, furnished rentals, value-add improvements, or even ancillary services such as parking or storage. By increasing income potential within each property, investors can enhance overall returns and improve financial resilience.

Market rotation is another advanced concept that involves shifting investments based on changing market conditions. Real estate markets are not static—some regions experience rapid appreciation, while others offer stronger cash flow or stability. By reallocating capital from one market to another, investors can take advantage of emerging opportunities and avoid stagnation. This requires ongoing market analysis and a willingness to adapt strategy over time. Risk diversification remains a cornerstone of long-term success. As portfolios expand, investors must ensure that they are not overly concentrated in a single market, property type, or economic segment. Diversifying across residential, multi-family, and even commercial assets can provide stability and reduce exposure to localized risks. Geographic diversification further enhances this stability by spreading investments across different regions.

Currency management becomes increasingly sophisticated at this level. Investors may use hedging strategies, maintain multi-currency accounts, or align income and expenses within the same currency to reduce exposure. For example, holding U.S. dollar-denominated assets and expenses can create a natural hedge, minimizing the impact of exchange rate fluctuations. Strategic currency management helps preserve gains and stabilize long-term performance.

Another powerful tool for advanced investors is portfolio consolidation. While scaling often involves acquiring multiple properties, there may come a point where consolidating assets into fewer, higher-value properties improves efficiency and reduces management complexity. This can also enhance borrowing capacity, as larger, more stable assets may qualify for more favorable financing terms.

Legacy planning is perhaps the most important aspect of advanced portfolio management. For many foreign national investors, real estate is not just a financial asset—it is a means of creating generational wealth. Structuring ownership in a way that facilitates transfer to heirs, minimizes legal complications, and preserves value is essential. This may involve trusts, succession planning, and coordination with legal advisors in multiple jurisdictions.

Operational excellence is another defining characteristic of advanced investors. Managing a large portfolio requires systems, processes, and reliable partnerships. Property management, accounting, legal compliance, and reporting must all be handled efficiently. Investors who build strong operational frameworks can scale more effectively and focus on strategic decision-making rather than day-to-day management.

Technology also plays a growing role in portfolio optimization. From property management software to financial tracking tools, technology enables investors to monitor performance, analyze data, and make informed decisions. Leveraging these tools enhances transparency and control, allowing investors to respond quickly to changes and opportunities.

Ultimately, advanced portfolio optimization is about

alignment. It is about ensuring that every asset, every loan, and every strategy works together toward a unified objective—whether that is income generation, capital appreciation, or long-term wealth preservation. Asset-based lending provides the flexibility needed to adapt and evolve, but it is the investor's strategy that determines success.

At this stage, the investor is no longer simply participating in the market—they are shaping their own financial ecosystem. By combining global structuring, strategic leverage, and disciplined management, foreign national borrowers can build portfolios that are not only profitable but sustainable and transferable across generations.

Real-Life Math Example: Advanced Portfolio Optimization and Global Structuring

To illustrate how these advanced strategies come together in practice, let us examine a detailed example of a foreign national investor optimizing a mature portfolio for efficiency and long-term growth.

Consider an investor named Hiroshi, based in Japan, who owns a portfolio of five U.S. properties with a combined value of $5,000,000. His total loan balance across these properties is $3,000,000, resulting in $2,000,000 in equity. The properties generate a combined rental income of $35,000 per month, with total monthly expenses of $24,000, resulting in a net cash flow of $11,000.

Hiroshi evaluates his portfolio and identifies that two properties have significantly appreciated but generate lower cash flow relative to their value. These properties are worth $1,800,000 combined and generate only $6,000 per month in net income. He decides to sell these properties and reinvest the capital into higher-performing assets.

After selling the properties, Hiroshi nets $1,600,000 after paying off associated loans and expenses. He allocates $800,000 as down payments on two multi-family properties valued at $2,500,000 combined. These new properties generate $20,000 per month in rental income, with expenses of $13,000, resulting in $7,000 in net cash flow.

Hiroshi also uses $400,000 to pay down existing loans, reducing his monthly expenses by $2,500. The remaining $400,000 is held in liquid reserves and investment accounts, providing flexibility for future opportunities.

After restructuring, Hiroshi's new portfolio consists of five properties with a combined value of $5,700,000 and a total loan balance of $3,100,000. His equity increases to $2,600,000. His total monthly rental income rises to $39,000, while expenses decrease to $23,500, resulting in a new net cash flow of $15,500 per month.

Additionally, Hiroshi restructures ownership through a holding company, improving tax efficiency and simplifying management. He also converts a portion of his income into U.S. dollars to reduce currency risk and align his financial flows.

Through these strategic adjustments, Hiroshi improves both the efficiency and performance of his portfolio. His cash flow increases, his equity grows, and his overall structure becomes more aligned with long-term goals.

This example demonstrates how advanced investors move beyond simple acquisition and focus on optimization. By analyzing performance, reallocating capital, and leveraging asset-based financing, they create portfolios that are dynamic, efficient, and resilient.

As you conclude this book, you now have a complete framework—from initial qualification to advanced portfolio optimization—for navigating the U.S. real estate market as a foreign national borrower. The principles outlined here are not just theoretical—they are practical tools that can be applied to build, scale, and sustain wealth over time. The next step is to implement these strategies with clarity, discipline, and a long-term vision for success.

Chapter 9

Risk Mitigation, Compliance, and Protecting Your Global Real Estate Investments

As foreign national investors build and optimize portfolios within the United States, one of the most critical responsibilities becomes protecting those investments against risk, regulatory exposure, and unforeseen disruptions. While asset-based mortgage lending provides access, flexibility, and scalability, long-term success depends on the ability to preserve capital, maintain compliance, and manage risk proactively. This chapter focuses on the systems, strategies, and mindset required to safeguard a global real estate portfolio in a complex and evolving financial environment.

Risk in real estate exists on multiple levels. There is market risk, where property values fluctuate due to economic conditions. There is operational risk, where tenant issues, maintenance costs, or management inefficiencies impact performance. There is financial risk, including interest rate changes, leverage exposure, and liquidity constraints. And for foreign national investors, there is an additional layer of cross-border risk involving currency fluctuations, regulatory differences, and legal complexities. Understanding these layers is the first step toward building a resilient portfolio.

Market risk is one of the most visible forms of exposure. Property values can rise or fall based on local economic conditions, supply and demand, and broader national trends. Foreign national investors must monitor these dynamics closely, especially when investing in unfamiliar markets. Diversifying across regions and property types can help reduce exposure to localized downturns. Investors who rely on a single market or asset class are more vulnerable to sudden changes, while diversified portfolios provide stability and balance.

Operational risk is often underestimated but can have a significant impact on performance. Property management plays a central role in mitigating this risk. Reliable property managers ensure that properties are maintained, tenants are properly screened, and rental income is collected consistently. For international investors, who may not be physically present, strong management is essential. Poor management can lead to vacancies, property damage, and financial losses, while effective management enhances stability and long-term value.

Financial risk is closely tied to leverage and loan structure. While leverage is a powerful tool for growth, it must be managed carefully. High levels of debt can amplify returns during strong markets, but they also increase vulnerability during downturns. Maintaining conservative loan-to-value ratios, strong reserves, and manageable payment structures helps reduce financial risk. Asset-based lending allows for flexibility, but discipline is required to avoid overextension.

Liquidity risk is another important consideration. Real estate is inherently illiquid, meaning it cannot be quickly converted into cash without potentially sacrificing value. Investors must ensure that they maintain sufficient liquid reserves to cover expenses, handle emergencies, and take advantage of new opportunities. Asset-based financing supports liquidity by allowing borrowers to leverage assets rather than liquidate them, but this must be balanced with prudent reserve management.

Compliance risk is particularly significant for foreign national investors. U.S. real estate transactions are subject to a range of federal, state, and local regulations, including tax reporting, anti-money laundering requirements, and property ownership laws. Failure to comply with these regulations can result in penalties, delays, or legal complications. Investors must work with qualified professionals to ensure that all aspects of their transactions and ongoing operations meet regulatory standards. One of the most important compliance areas is the verification of funds. Lenders and regulatory bodies require clear documentation of the source of funds used in transactions. This includes tracing the origin of funds, ensuring they are legally obtained, and verifying that they are not connected to prohibited activities. For foreign nationals, this process often involves additional documentation and scrutiny, making transparency and organization essential.

Tax compliance is another critical area. Foreign investors are subject to specific tax rules when buying, holding, and selling U.S. real estate. This includes withholding requirements at the time of sale and ongoing reporting obligations. Understanding these rules—and planning accordingly—can prevent unexpected liabilities and protect overall returns. Strategic tax planning is not just about minimizing costs; it is about ensuring compliance and avoiding future complications.

Legal structuring plays a key role in risk mitigation. Holding properties through appropriate entities can provide liability protection and simplify ownership. For example, limited liability companies can shield personal assets from property-related risks, while holding companies can centralize management and streamline operations. The right structure depends on individual circumstances, but it should always align with both legal requirements and investment goals. Insurance is another essential tool for protecting real estate investments. Property insurance covers physical damage, while liability insurance protects against claims related to injuries or other incidents. For foreign national investors, it is important to ensure that coverage is comprehensive and tailored to the specific risks associated with each property. Adequate insurance provides a safety net that supports long-term stability.

Currency risk remains a constant factor in cross-border investing. Exchange rate fluctuations can impact both asset values and cash flow. Investors must consider how currency movements affect their overall portfolio and may choose to implement strategies such as maintaining U.S. dollar accounts or aligning income and expenses within the same currency. Managing currency exposure helps preserve gains and reduce volatility.

Another important aspect of risk mitigation is contingency planning. Investors should prepare for unexpected events such as economic downturns, vacancies, or changes in regulations. This includes maintaining reserves, diversifying income streams, and having clear plans for managing challenges. A proactive approach to risk ensures that investors are not caught off guard and can respond effectively to changing conditions.

Technology and data analysis also play a growing role in risk management. By monitoring performance metrics, tracking market trends, and analyzing financial data, investors can make informed decisions and identify potential issues early. This level of insight allows for more precise and timely adjustments, enhancing overall portfolio resilience.

Ultimately, risk mitigation is not about eliminating risk—it is about managing it intelligently. Every investment carries some level of uncertainty, but with the right strategies, systems, and mindset, that risk can be controlled and even leveraged to create opportunity. For foreign national investors, this means combining global awareness with local expertise to build a portfolio that is both dynamic and secure.

Real-Life Math Example: Risk Management, Reserves, and Portfolio Protection

To demonstrate how risk mitigation strategies are applied in practice, let us examine a detailed example of a foreign national investor managing financial exposure and protecting a growing portfolio.

Consider an investor named Ana, based in Argentina, who owns four U.S. properties with a combined value of

$3,200,000. Her total loan balance is $2,000,000, resulting in $1,200,000 in equity. The properties generate a combined rental income of $24,000 per month, with total expenses of $17,000, resulting in a net cash flow of $7,000. Ana evaluates her portfolio and identifies potential risks. First, her loan-to-value ratio is approximately 62.5%, which is moderate but could become a concern if property values decline. Second, she holds most of her reserves in her home currency, which has experienced volatility. Third, one of her properties has higher vacancy rates, impacting overall cash flow.

To address these risks, Ana implements several strategies. She allocates $200,000 from her assets to pay down a portion of her loans, reducing her total loan balance to $1,800,000. This lowers her loan-to-value ratio to approximately 56%, improving stability and reducing financial risk.

Next, Ana converts $150,000 of her reserves into U.S. dollars and places them in a U.S. account. This aligns her reserves with her expenses and reduces currency exposure. She now maintains 12 months of reserves, equal to $204,000 (12 months of $17,000 expenses), providing a strong safety buffer.

To address operational risk, Ana invests $50,000 in improvements to the underperforming property, increasing its rental income from $4,500 to $6,000 per month. This boosts overall portfolio income and reduces vacancy risk.

After implementing these changes, Ana's portfolio generates $25,500 per month in rental income, with expenses reduced to $16,500 due to lower debt payments. Her net cash flow increases to $9,000 per month, while her risk exposure decreases significantly.

Ana also ensures compliance by working with tax and legal professionals to confirm that her ownership structure and reporting meet all requirements. She updates her insurance coverage to reflect the increased value of her properties and implements regular performance monitoring using financial tracking tools.

Through these adjustments, Ana transforms her portfolio into a more stable and resilient system. She reduces financial risk, improves cash flow, and strengthens her overall position. This example demonstrates that risk management is not a one-time action, but an ongoing process that requires attention, strategy, and adaptability.

As you continue to refine your approach, remember that protecting your investments is just as important as acquiring them. By combining strong risk mitigation strategies with asset-based financing, you can build a portfolio that not only grows but endures.

Chapter 10

Building a Global Real Estate Empire with Asset-Based Mortgage Strategies

Reaching the final stage of this journey is not about ending the process—it is about stepping into a new level of vision, control, and execution. At this point, foreign national investors are no longer simply learning how to qualify, acquire, or even scale. They are now in a position to build a true global real estate empire—one that is structured, systemized, and designed for long-term dominance, stability, and generational wealth. This chapter brings together everything you have learned and elevates it into a cohesive strategy for creating a powerful, asset-driven financial ecosystem.

The concept of a real estate empire is not defined by the number of properties alone. It is defined by control, leverage, efficiency, and sustainability. It is about owning assets that produce income, appreciate over time, and can be strategically leveraged to create new opportunities. For foreign national investors, this empire is uniquely powerful because it bridges global capital with one of the most stable and dynamic real estate markets in the world—the United States. At the core of building an empire is vision. Without a clear long-term objective, even the most successful transactions can become isolated events rather than part of a larger strategy. Investors must define what success looks like—whether it is a specific level of monthly cash flow, a target portfolio value, or the creation of a legacy asset base for future generations. This vision becomes the foundation for every decision moving forward.

Systemization is the next critical step. An empire cannot be built on isolated efforts—it requires systems that allow for consistency, scalability, and efficiency. This includes standardized processes for acquiring properties, managing assets, handling finances, and evaluating performance. Investors who develop repeatable systems can scale faster and with greater control, reducing reliance on ad hoc decisions.

Leverage remains the driving force behind expansion. Asset-based mortgage strategies allow investors to use existing assets to acquire new ones without liquidating capital. This creates a compounding effect, where each asset contributes to the growth of the next. However, leverage must be used strategically. Over-leveraging can create vulnerability, while disciplined leverage enhances growth and stability. The goal is to find the balance that maximizes opportunity while maintaining control.

Capital allocation becomes increasingly important at this stage. Investors must decide how to distribute resources across acquisitions, reserves, improvements, and new opportunities. Every dollar should have a purpose, whether it is generating income, preserving liquidity, or supporting future growth. Efficient capital allocation ensures that the portfolio remains dynamic and responsive to changing conditions.

Another defining characteristic of a real estate empire is diversification at scale. This includes not only geographic diversification but also diversification across property types and income streams. Residential properties, multi-family units, and even select commercial assets can all play a role in creating a balanced portfolio. Each asset class contributes differently, providing a mix of stability, cash flow, and appreciation.

Operational infrastructure becomes a cornerstone of success. Managing a large portfolio requires a network of professionals, including property managers, accountants, legal advisors, and financial strategists. These individuals form the backbone of the empire, ensuring that operations run smoothly and efficiently. Investors who build strong teams can focus on strategy and growth rather than day-to-day management.

Data-driven decision-making is another critical element. At

this level, intuition alone is not enough. Investors must rely on data to evaluate performance, identify trends, and make informed decisions. This includes tracking key metrics such as cash flow, return on equity, occupancy rates, and market conditions. Technology plays a significant role here, providing tools for monitoring and analysis.

Global integration is what sets foreign national investors apart. By operating across borders, they have access to diverse capital sources, markets, and opportunities. This allows for strategic positioning that domestic investors may not be able to replicate. For example, capital generated in one country can be deployed in another, creating a flow of resources that enhances overall growth.

Another important aspect is resilience. Markets change, economic conditions fluctuate, and unexpected events occur. A true real estate empire is designed to withstand these challenges. This includes maintaining strong reserves, diversifying risk, and continuously adapting strategy. Resilience ensures that the empire not only grows but endures over time.

Legacy creation is the ultimate goal. Beyond financial returns, a real estate empire represents a lasting impact. It is something that can be passed down, expanded, and used to support future generations. Structuring the portfolio with this in mind—through proper legal entities, succession planning, and strategic management—ensures that the value created today continues into the future. Continuous learning and adaptation are also essential. The real estate market is constantly evolving, and successful investors evolve with it. This means staying informed, refining strategies, and embracing new opportunities. Asset-based lending itself is an example of how innovation can transform the way investors approach financing and growth.

Ultimately, building a global real estate empire is about alignment. It is about aligning vision, strategy, capital, and execution into a unified system that drives long-term success. Asset-based mortgage strategies provide the foundation, but it is the investor's discipline, creativity, and commitment that bring it to life.

At this stage, the investor is no longer reacting to opportunities—they are creating them. They are not limited by traditional constraints—they are operating within a framework that allows for flexibility, scalability, and control. This is the true power of asset-based lending and global real estate investing.

Real-Life Math Example: Building and Scaling a Global Real Estate Empire

To illustrate how these principles come together in practice, let us examine a comprehensive example of a foreign national investor building a large-scale real estate portfolio using asset-based mortgage strategies.

Consider an investor named David, based in Canada, with $5,000,000 in qualifying assets. David's goal is to build a portfolio that generates $50,000 per month in net cash flow within five years. He begins by allocating his capital strategically, ensuring that he maintains sufficient reserves while maximizing leverage.

In the first year, David acquires three properties with a combined value of $3,000,000. He puts down 30%, or $900,000, resulting in a total loan amount of $2,100,000. After these acquisitions, he has $4,100,000 in remaining assets.

The properties generate a combined rental income of $21,000 per month, with expenses of $15,000, resulting in a net cash flow of $6,000. David reinvests this cash flow into his portfolio, increasing his available capital over time.

In the second year, David uses an additional $800,000 for down payments on two more properties valued at $2,500,000.

His total portfolio value now reaches $5,500,000, with a combined loan balance of $3,800,000. His total monthly rental income increases to $35,000, with expenses of $25,000, resulting in a net cash flow of $10,000. By the third year, David leverages appreciation and refinancing to extract $500,000 in equity from his existing properties. He uses this capital, along with additional assets, to acquire three more properties valued at $3,500,000. His portfolio now includes eight properties with a total value of $9,000,000.

At this stage, his total monthly rental income is $58,000, with expenses of $41,000, resulting in a net cash flow of $17,000. He continues to reinvest cash flow and optimize his portfolio through strategic refinancing and asset reallocation.

By the fifth year, David's portfolio grows to $15,000,000 in total value, with a loan balance of $10,000,000 and equity of $5,000,000. His monthly rental income reaches $95,000, with expenses of $45,000, resulting in a net cash flow of $50,000—achieving his original goal.

Throughout this process, David maintains strong reserves, diversifies across markets, and continuously optimizes his portfolio. He structures his holdings through appropriate entities, manages currency exposure, and builds a professional team to support operations.

This example demonstrates the power of combining vision, strategy, and asset-based financing. By leveraging assets, reinvesting income, and scaling systematically, David transforms his initial capital into a large and sustainable real estate empire. As you complete this series, you now have a complete roadmap—from understanding asset-based lending to building a global portfolio and optimizing it for long-term success. The next step is to take action, apply these strategies, and begin building your own real estate empire with clarity, confidence, and purpose.

Chapter 11

Building Systems, Automation, and a Self-Sustaining Real Estate Machine

At the highest level of real estate investing, success is no longer measured by how many deals you can personally manage, but by how effectively you can create systems that operate without constant involvement. For foreign national investors, this concept is even more critical. Distance, time zones, and cross-border logistics make it impractical to manage every detail manually. The solution is to build a self-sustaining real estate machine—one powered by systems, automation, and strategic delegation.

The transition from investor to system builder represents a major shift in mindset. Instead of asking, "How do I close this deal?" the question becomes, "How do I build a process that closes deals consistently?" This shift is what allows portfolios to scale beyond personal limitations. Asset-based mortgage strategies provide the financial foundation, but systems provide the operational engine.

The first system to build is the acquisition system. This includes identifying target markets, sourcing deals, analyzing opportunities, and securing financing. A strong acquisition system relies on repeatable criteria. For example, an investor may define specific parameters such as property price range, minimum cash flow, location characteristics, and acceptable loan terms. By standardizing these criteria, the investor can quickly evaluate opportunities and make consistent decisions.

Lead generation is a key component of the acquisition system. This may involve working with real estate agents, wholesalers, or online platforms that provide access to deals. For foreign national investors, building relationships with local professionals is essential. These individuals act as the investor's eyes and ears on the ground, identifying opportunities and providing market insights.

Once a deal is identified, the analysis system comes into play. This involves evaluating the financial performance of the property, including rental income, expenses, and potential appreciation. Investors who rely on structured analysis tools—such as spreadsheets or software—can quickly determine whether a property meets their criteria. This reduces emotional decision-making and ensures consistency.

The financing system is another critical component. Asset-based lending requires coordination with lenders, documentation preparation, and timeline management. By creating a standardized process for submitting applications, organizing documents, and communicating with lenders, investors can streamline this stage and reduce delays. Over time, relationships with lenders can further enhance efficiency and access to capital.

After acquisition, the focus shifts to the management system. This includes property management, tenant relations, maintenance, and financial tracking. For foreign national investors, professional property management is often the cornerstone of this system. A reliable management company handles day-to-day operations, allowing the investor to focus on strategy rather than execution.

Financial management is another essential system. This involves tracking income, expenses, loan payments, and overall portfolio performance. Investors must maintain clear and accurate records to evaluate profitability and make informed decisions. Automation tools can simplify this process, providing real-time insights into financial performance.

Automation plays a powerful role in creating efficiency. Tasks such as rent collection, expense tracking, and reporting can be automated through technology. This reduces manual work and minimizes the risk of errors. For example, automated payment systems ensure that rent is collected consistently, while financial software can generate reports that provide a clear overview of performance.

Communication systems are also critical, especially for international investors. Clear and consistent communication with property managers, lenders, and advisors ensures that issues are addressed promptly and that operations run smoothly. Establishing regular reporting schedules and communication protocols helps maintain alignment across all parties.

Another important system is the scaling system. As the portfolio grows, investors must ensure that their processes can handle increased volume. This may involve expanding the team, upgrading technology, or refining workflows. Scaling is not just about doing more—it is about doing more efficiently.

Risk management systems must also be integrated into the overall structure. This includes monitoring reserves, tracking market conditions, and maintaining compliance with legal and financial requirements. By embedding risk management into daily operations, investors can identify potential issues early and respond proactively.

Performance optimization is the final layer of the system. This involves continuously evaluating the portfolio and identifying opportunities for improvement. Whether through refinancing, property upgrades, or market repositioning, optimization ensures that the portfolio remains aligned with the investor's goals.

One of the most powerful outcomes of building systems is time freedom. When operations are automated and delegated, investors are no longer tied to the day-to-day management of their portfolio. This allows them to focus on higher-level strategy, explore new opportunities, and maintain a balanced lifestyle.

For foreign national investors, systems also provide consistency across borders. Regardless of location, the portfolio operates according to predefined processes, ensuring stability and predictability. This is especially valuable when managing properties in a different country.

Ultimately, building a self-sustaining real estate machine is about creating a structure that supports long-term growth. It is about transforming individual actions into repeatable processes and leveraging technology and partnerships to achieve scale. Asset-based lending provides the fuel, but systems provide the engine that drives the entire operation.

Real-Life Math Example: Systemized Scaling and Automated Portfolio Growth

To demonstrate how systems and automation impact real-world performance, let us examine a detailed example of a foreign national investor building a systemized portfolio.

Consider an investor named Sofia, based in Chile, with $3,000,000 in qualifying assets. Sofia's goal is to build a portfolio that generates $30,000 per month in net cash flow while minimizing active involvement.

In the first phase, Sofia establishes her acquisition criteria: properties between $400,000 and $800,000, minimum net cash flow of $500 per property, and locations with strong rental demand. She partners with a local real estate agent who provides a steady flow of opportunities.

Using her criteria, Sofia acquires four properties in the first year with a combined value of $2,400,000. She puts down 30%, or $720,000, resulting in a loan amount of $1,680,000. After these acquisitions, she has $2,280,000 in remaining assets.

Each property generates an average of $6,000 in monthly rental income, with expenses of $5,200, resulting in $800 in net cash flow per property. Across four properties, Sofia generates $3,200 per month in net cash flow. Sofia implements an automated management system, where rent collection, expense tracking, and reporting are handled through software. Her property manager provides monthly updates, allowing her to monitor performance without direct involvement.

In the second year, Sofia uses her remaining assets to acquire three additional properties valued at $2,100,000. She invests $630,000 in down payments, maintaining strong reserves. Her portfolio now includes seven properties with a total value of $4,500,000.

Her total monthly rental income increases to $42,000, with expenses of $35,000, resulting in a net cash flow of $7,000. Automation ensures that operations remain consistent despite the increased scale.

In the third year, Sofia leverages refinancing to extract $300,000 in equity, which she uses to acquire two more properties. Her portfolio grows to nine properties with a total value of $6,000,000.

At this stage, her monthly rental income reaches $56,000, with expenses of $44,000, resulting in a net cash flow of $12,000. Her systems allow her to manage this growth without increasing her workload significantly.

By the fifth year, Sofia's portfolio expands to 15 properties with a total value of $10,000,000. Her monthly rental income reaches $90,000, with expenses of $60,000, resulting in a net cash flow of $30,000—achieving her original goal.

Throughout this process, Sofia relies on systems and automation to maintain efficiency. Her acquisition criteria, management processes, and financial tracking systems ensure consistency and scalability. She spends her time on strategy rather than operations, allowing her to continue growing her portfolio.

This example demonstrates that success in real estate is not just about numbers—it is about systems. By building a structured and automated approach, investors can achieve scale, efficiency, and long-term success without being overwhelmed by complexity.

As you continue your journey, remember that the ultimate goal is not just to build a portfolio, but to build a machine that sustains and grows that portfolio over time.

Chapter 12

Mastery, Control, and the Long-Term Evolution of a Global Asset-Based Real Estate Strategy

Reaching this stage is not simply about having knowledge—it is about mastery. Mastery is the ability to see the entire system, anticipate outcomes, and make decisions with clarity and precision. For foreign national investors using asset-based mortgage strategies, mastery represents the transition from participation to control. It is the point where you are no longer reacting to opportunities—you are engineering them. This chapter focuses on the long-term evolution of your strategy, how to maintain control as your portfolio grows, and how to position yourself for sustained success across decades.

At the highest level, mastery begins with perspective. Instead of viewing each property or loan as an isolated transaction, you begin to see your portfolio as an interconnected system. Every decision—whether it involves acquisition, refinancing, or asset allocation—affects the overall structure. This systems-level thinking allows you to optimize not just individual components, but the entire portfolio. Control is the defining characteristic of mastery. Control does not mean eliminating uncertainty—it means managing it effectively. It means understanding your numbers, knowing your risk exposure, and having the ability to adjust your strategy as conditions change. For foreign national investors, control also involves navigating cross-border complexities, including currency management, regulatory compliance, and global financial flows.

One of the key elements of long-term strategy is adaptability. Markets evolve, interest rates fluctuate, and economic conditions shift. Investors who succeed over decades are those who can adapt without losing sight of their core objectives. Asset-based lending provides the flexibility needed to adjust financing structures, access capital, and reposition assets as needed. This adaptability is a major advantage in a dynamic global environment.

Another critical component is capital preservation. While growth is important, protecting what you have built is equally essential. This involves maintaining strong reserves, managing leverage carefully, and avoiding unnecessary risk. Preservation ensures that your portfolio can withstand downturns and continue to generate value over time.

Strategic patience is another hallmark of mastery. Not every opportunity needs to be pursued, and not every market condition requires action. Knowing when to act—and when to wait—is a skill that develops over time. Investors who exercise patience often achieve better outcomes by avoiding overextension and focusing on high-quality opportunities.

Long-term planning also involves aligning your portfolio with your personal and financial goals. This includes defining your desired level of involvement, your income targets, and your legacy objectives. By aligning your strategy with your goals, you create a sense of direction and purpose that guides your decisions.

Another important aspect is continuous optimization. Even a well-performing portfolio can be improved. This may involve refinancing to reduce costs, upgrading properties to increase income, or reallocating capital to higher-performing assets. Optimization is an ongoing process that ensures your portfolio remains efficient and competitive.

Global awareness is essential for foreign national investors. Economic conditions, regulatory changes, and market trends in different countries can all impact your portfolio. Staying informed and maintaining a global perspective allows you to anticipate changes and position yourself accordingly.

Leadership also becomes a key factor at this stage. As your portfolio grows, you are no longer working alone—you are leading a team of professionals who support your operations. Effective leadership ensures that your team is aligned with your goals and that your systems function smoothly. This includes clear communication, defined roles, and accountability.

Another advanced concept is strategic simplification. As portfolios grow, complexity can increase. While diversification is important, excessive complexity can reduce efficiency and increase risk. Simplifying your structure—whether through consolidation, standardization, or improved systems—can enhance control and performance.

Time becomes one of the most valuable assets at this level. The goal is not just to generate income, but to create a system that allows you to use your time effectively. This may involve delegating operational tasks, automating processes, and focusing on high-level strategy. Time freedom is one of the ultimate benefits of a well-structured real estate portfolio.

Legacy thinking continues to play a central role. Mastery involves not just building wealth, but ensuring that it can be transferred, sustained, and expanded by future generations. This requires thoughtful planning, clear structures, and a long-term perspective.

Another important element is resilience. Even the most well-structured portfolios will face challenges. Market downturns, unexpected expenses, or changes in regulations can create pressure. Resilience comes from preparation—strong reserves, diversified assets, and a flexible strategy. Investors who build resilience into their systems are better equipped to navigate uncertainty.

Finally, mastery is about confidence. Not overconfidence, but informed confidence—the ability to make decisions based on knowledge, experience, and a clear understanding of your strategy. This confidence allows you to act decisively, adapt effectively, and maintain control even in uncertain conditions.

At this stage, your role as an investor evolves. You are no longer just acquiring properties or managing loans—you are designing a financial ecosystem that operates with precision and purpose. Asset-based mortgage strategies provide the framework, but mastery is what brings it to life.

Real-Life Math Example: Long-Term Portfolio Control and Optimization Over Time

To illustrate how mastery and long-term strategy work in practice, let us examine a detailed example of a foreign national investor managing and optimizing a mature portfolio over time.

Consider an investor named Lucas, based in Brazil, who has built a portfolio of 12 U.S. properties with a total value of $12,000,000. His total loan balance is $7,500,000, resulting in $4,500,000 in equity. The portfolio generates $90,000 per month in rental income, with expenses of $60,000, resulting in a net cash flow of $30,000.

Lucas evaluates his portfolio and identifies opportunities for optimization. First, he notices that interest rates have decreased since he acquired several of his properties. He decides to refinance $5,000,000 of his loans at a lower rate, reducing his monthly payments by $5,000.

Next, Lucas identifies two properties that are underperforming relative to their value. These properties are worth $2,000,000 combined and generate only $6,000 per month in net income. He sells these properties and nets $1,800,000 after expenses and loan payoffs.

Lucas reinvests $1,000,000 of this capital into two higher-performing properties valued at $3,000,000 combined. These new properties generate $18,000 per month in net income, significantly improving overall performance. He retains $800,000 as reserves and for future opportunities.

After these adjustments, Lucas's portfolio consists of 12 properties with a total value of $13,000,000. His loan balance is $7,800,000, and his equity increases to $5,200,000. His monthly rental income rises to $102,000, while expenses decrease to $58,000, resulting in a new net cash flow of $44,000. Lucas also restructures his portfolio to simplify management, consolidating ownership under a single holding company. This improves efficiency and reduces administrative complexity. He aligns his currency strategy by maintaining U.S. dollar accounts for income and expenses, reducing exchange rate risk.

Over the next five years, Lucas continues to optimize his portfolio, reinvesting cash flow, refinancing strategically, and adjusting his holdings based on market conditions. His portfolio grows to $18,000,000 in value, with a loan balance of $10,000,000 and equity of $8,000,000. His monthly net cash flow reaches $60,000.

Through disciplined management, strategic decisions, and continuous optimization, Lucas achieves long-term control over his portfolio. He is no longer focused on individual transactions, but on maintaining and evolving a system that generates consistent income and growth.

This example demonstrates that mastery is not a destination—it is an ongoing process. By applying the principles outlined in this chapter, investors can maintain control, adapt to changing conditions, and continue building wealth over time.

As you complete this book, you now possess a complete framework for navigating every stage of foreign national asset-based mortgage lending—from qualification and acquisition to scaling, optimization, and mastery. The final step is to apply these principles with discipline, clarity, and a long-term vision for success.

Chapter 13

Advanced Deal Structuring, Creative Financing, and Unlocking Hidden Opportunities

At this stage of your journey, you have moved beyond simply qualifying, acquiring, and scaling. You now understand the system, the numbers, and the strategies. Chapter 13 takes you into the next level—where deals are not just found, but engineered. This is where advanced investors separate themselves from the average by structuring opportunities that others either overlook or cannot execute. It is no longer about waiting for the perfect deal; it is about creating one.

Advanced deal structuring begins with understanding that every transaction has multiple layers. Price is only one component. Terms, timing, financing structure, asset positioning, and even negotiation strategy all play a role in determining whether a deal is profitable. For foreign national investors using asset-based lending, this flexibility creates powerful opportunities to structure deals in ways that maximize returns while minimizing risk.

One of the most important concepts is value creation. Many investors focus only on properties that are already performing well, but advanced investors look for properties with unrealized potential. This may include under-rented units, outdated properties that can be improved, or assets located in areas with strong future growth. By identifying and unlocking this potential, investors can create equity and increase income, transforming an average deal into a high-performing asset.

Creative financing is another key component of advanced structuring. While asset-based mortgages provide a strong foundation, they can be combined with other strategies to enhance flexibility. This may include seller concessions, partial financing arrangements, or structuring deals that reduce upfront capital requirements. The goal is not just to secure financing, but to optimize how capital is deployed.

Negotiation plays a critical role in this process. Many deals are won or lost based on how effectively terms are negotiated. This includes not only the purchase price, but also closing timelines, contingencies, and concessions. For foreign national investors, demonstrating financial strength through asset-based pre-approval can significantly enhance negotiating power, making sellers more willing to accept favorable terms.

Another advanced strategy is identifying off-market opportunities. These are properties that are not publicly listed but are available through direct relationships or specialized networks. Off-market deals often provide better pricing and less competition, allowing investors to acquire assets at more favorable terms. Building relationships with local professionals is key to accessing these opportunities.

Timing is another critical factor. Market conditions, interest rates, and seller motivations all influence the structure of a deal. Advanced investors understand how to align their strategy with these factors. For example, in a slower market, sellers may be more willing to negotiate, while in a competitive market, speed and certainty become more important.

Portfolio integration is also an important consideration. Each new acquisition should fit within the broader strategy of the portfolio. This includes evaluating how the property contributes to cash flow, diversification, and overall performance. Advanced investors do not view deals in isolation—they consider how each acquisition strengthens the entire system.

Risk-adjusted returns are another key concept. Not all high-return opportunities are worth pursuing if they carry excessive risk. Advanced investors evaluate deals based on both potential returns and associated risks, ensuring that the overall portfolio remains balanced and sustainable.

Another powerful approach is combining acquisition with repositioning. This involves purchasing a property and immediately implementing improvements or changes that increase its value. This could include renovations, rent adjustments, or operational improvements. By increasing value quickly, investors can create equity that can be leveraged for future growth.

Foreign national investors also have the advantage of global capital flexibility. They can allocate funds across markets, currencies, and asset classes, allowing them to pursue opportunities that align with their strategy. This flexibility can be a significant advantage when structuring deals.

Another important element is exit alignment. Every deal should be structured with an exit strategy in mind. Whether the goal is to sell, refinance, or hold long-term, the initial structure should support that objective. This ensures that the investment remains aligned with the investor's broader goals.

Technology and data also play a role in advanced deal structuring. By analyzing market trends, property performance, and financial metrics, investors can identify opportunities and make informed decisions. Data-driven analysis enhances accuracy and reduces uncertainty.

Ultimately, advanced deal structuring is about creativity and control. It is about seeing opportunities where others see limitations and using strategy to turn those opportunities into profitable investments. Asset-based lending provides the flexibility needed to execute these strategies, but it is the investor's vision and execution that bring them to life.

At this level, you are no longer just participating in the market—you are shaping your own opportunities. This is where real wealth is created.

Real-Life Math Example: Structuring a Value-Add Deal with Creative Financing

To illustrate how advanced deal structuring works in practice, let us examine a detailed example of a foreign national investor creating value through strategic structuring.

Consider an investor named Daniel, based in Spain, with $2,200,000 in qualifying assets. Daniel identifies a multi-family property in Texas listed at $1,200,000. The property is underperforming, generating only $7,000 per month in rental income, while similar properties in the area generate closer to $10,000.

Daniel negotiates the purchase price down to $1,100,000 due to the property's underperformance. He also negotiates a $50,000 seller credit to cover part of the renovation costs. He plans to put down 30%, or $330,000, resulting in a loan amount of $770,000. After applying asset eligibility adjustments, Daniel has $1,600,000 in qualifying assets remaining. Using asset depletion over 60 months, his qualifying income is approximately $26,666 per month.

His initial monthly housing expense is $6,800. Combined with the current rental income of $7,000, the property is near break-even. However, Daniel plans to invest $100,000 in renovations to increase rental income.

After renovations, the property's rental income increases to $10,000 per month. Expenses remain at $6,800, resulting in a net cash flow of $3,200 per month.

The increased income also raises the property's value. Based on a capitalization rate of 6%, the property's new value is approximately $2,000,000 ($10,000 monthly income equates to $120,000 annually, divided by 0.06). This creates nearly $900,000 in equity.

Daniel then refinances the property at 70% loan-to-value based on the new value. This allows him to obtain a new loan of $1,400,000. After paying off the original loan of $770,000, he extracts $630,000 in cash.

Daniel uses this capital to acquire another property, repeating the process. Through strategic structuring, negotiation, and value creation, he transforms a single underperforming asset into a powerful engine for growth. This example demonstrates how advanced investors create opportunities rather than simply finding them. By combining asset-based lending with creative structuring, they unlock value and accelerate portfolio growth.

As you continue your journey, remember that the most powerful deals are often the ones you create.

Chapter 14

Creating Predictable Deal Flow, Building Strategic Partnerships, and Operating at Scale

At this stage in your evolution as a foreign national real estate investor, the challenge is no longer understanding the strategy or even executing individual deals—it is consistency. The difference between an investor who occasionally succeeds and one who builds a true empire is the ability to generate predictable deal flow, leverage strategic partnerships, and operate at scale with precision. Chapter 14 is about building the infrastructure that feeds your portfolio continuously and allows you to grow without relying on chance or sporadic opportunities.

Predictable deal flow is the lifeblood of a scalable real estate operation. Without it, growth becomes inconsistent and reactive. Many investors spend too much time waiting for deals instead of building systems that bring deals to them. At an advanced level, deal flow must be engineered. This involves creating multiple channels through which opportunities are sourced, evaluated, and executed. One of the most effective ways to create deal flow is through relationships. Real estate is a relationship-driven business, and those who build strong networks gain access to opportunities that are not available to the general market. This includes real estate agents, brokers, wholesalers, developers, and even other investors. Each of these relationships can serve as a source of deals, insights, and strategic advantages.

For foreign national investors, partnerships are even more critical. Being physically removed from the market means that you must rely on trusted individuals on the ground. These partners act as extensions of your operation, identifying opportunities, conducting due diligence, and facilitating transactions. Choosing the right partners is one of the most important decisions you will make, as their performance directly impacts your results.

Another key component of deal flow is marketing. While many investors rely solely on agents or listings, advanced investors often create their own opportunities through targeted marketing efforts. This can include direct outreach to property owners, digital advertising, or specialized campaigns aimed at identifying motivated sellers. By generating inbound opportunities, you reduce competition and increase control over the deal pipeline. Technology plays a significant role in managing deal flow. Tools that aggregate listings, analyze market data, and track opportunities allow investors to operate more efficiently. By centralizing information and automating parts of the process, you can evaluate more deals in less time and make faster decisions. This is especially important when operating across borders, where efficiency becomes a competitive advantage.

Once deal flow is established, the next step is creating a filtering system. Not every opportunity is worth pursuing, and advanced investors must be highly selective. This involves defining clear criteria for what constitutes a viable deal. These criteria may include minimum cash flow, acceptable risk levels, location preferences, and alignment with long-term strategy. By applying these filters consistently, you ensure that only the most relevant opportunities move forward.

Strategic partnerships extend beyond deal sourcing. They also play a role in financing, management, and optimization. Lenders, for example, are not just providers of capital—they are strategic partners who can influence your ability to scale. Building strong relationships with lenders who understand asset-based financing can improve access to capital and streamline future transactions.

Property management partnerships are equally important. As your portfolio grows, the quality of your management team directly impacts performance. A strong property manager not only maintains the property but also maximizes income, reduces vacancies, and enhances tenant satisfaction. This contributes to both cash flow and long-term value.

Another critical partnership is with financial and legal advisors. These professionals ensure that your operations remain compliant and optimized. They provide guidance on structuring, taxation, and risk management, helping you navigate the complexities of cross-border investing.

Operating at scale requires a shift in mindset. At a smaller level, investors can rely on manual processes and direct involvement. At scale, this approach becomes inefficient and unsustainable. Systems, automation, and delegation become essential. Every aspect of your operation—from deal sourcing to property management—must be designed to handle increased volume without sacrificing quality.

Standardization is a key element of scaling. By creating standardized processes for evaluating deals, submitting loan applications, and managing properties, you reduce variability and improve efficiency. This allows your operation to grow without becoming chaotic or disorganized.

Another important concept is pipeline management. Deals move through different stages—from initial identification to analysis, negotiation, and closing. Managing this pipeline effectively ensures that opportunities are tracked, prioritized, and executed in a timely manner. This prevents deals from falling through the cracks and maximizes conversion rates.

Capital deployment also becomes more strategic at this level. With a steady flow of opportunities, investors must decide how to allocate resources efficiently. This includes balancing new acquisitions with reserves, refinancing opportunities, and portfolio optimization. Effective capital deployment ensures that growth is sustainable and aligned with long-term goals.

Risk management remains a constant consideration. As deal flow increases, so does the potential for mistakes or oversight. Maintaining discipline in evaluation and adhering to established criteria helps mitigate this risk. Scaling should never come at the expense of quality.

Another powerful aspect of predictable deal flow is negotiation leverage. When you have multiple opportunities in your pipeline, you are not dependent on any single deal. This allows you to negotiate from a position of strength, securing better terms and avoiding unfavorable conditions. Abundance creates leverage.

Foreign national investors also benefit from global perspective. By comparing opportunities across markets and understanding different economic conditions, they can identify where capital is most effectively deployed. This global view enhances decision-making and creates additional opportunities.

Ultimately, creating predictable deal flow and operating at scale is about building a system that continuously generates and executes opportunities. It is about moving from a reactive approach to a proactive one, where you control the flow of deals rather than waiting for them.

This is where your operation becomes a true business. It is no longer dependent on individual transactions—it is driven by systems, partnerships, and strategy. Asset-based lending provides the financial engine, but deal flow and partnerships provide the fuel that keeps it running.

Real-Life Math Example: Building a Predictable Deal Flow System and Scaling Efficiently

To demonstrate how predictable deal flow and scaling work in practice, let us examine a detailed example of a foreign national investor building a systemized acquisition pipeline.

Consider an investor named Victor, based in Colombia, with $3,500,000 in qualifying assets. Victor's goal is to acquire 10 properties within three years while maintaining strong cash flow and reserves. Victor begins by building relationships with three real estate agents, two wholesalers, and one property manager in his target market. Each partner provides a steady stream of opportunities. On average, Victor receives 20 potential deals per month.

Using his filtering criteria, Victor narrows these down to five viable opportunities. He conducts detailed analysis on these properties and selects one to pursue each month. This results in 12 acquisitions per year, although he plans to close on fewer to maintain quality.

In the first year, Victor acquires four properties with a combined value of $2,800,000. He puts down 30%, or $840,000, resulting in a loan amount of $1,960,000. After these acquisitions, he has $2,660,000 in remaining assets.

Each property generates an average of $7,000 in monthly rental income, with expenses of $5,800, resulting in $1,200 in net cash flow per property. Across four properties, Victor generates $4,800 per month in net cash flow.

In the second year, Victor continues to leverage his deal flow system and acquires three additional properties valued at $2,100,000. His portfolio now includes seven properties with a total value of $4,900,000.

His total monthly rental income increases to $49,000, with expenses of $38,000, resulting in a net cash flow of $11,000.

His pipeline remains active, ensuring a continuous flow of opportunities.

By the third year, Victor refines his system further, improving efficiency and conversion rates. He acquires three more properties, reaching his goal of 10 properties with a total value of $7,000,000.

At this stage, his monthly rental income reaches $70,000, with expenses of $52,000, resulting in a net cash flow of $18,000. His systems and partnerships allow him to manage this portfolio effectively without increasing his workload significantly.

Victor's success is not based on luck—it is based on a system. By creating predictable deal flow, leveraging partnerships, and operating at scale, he builds a portfolio that grows consistently and sustainably.

This example demonstrates that the key to scaling is not just finding deals—it is creating a system that produces them. When deal flow becomes predictable, growth becomes inevitable.

As you continue your journey, focus on building systems that support consistency. This is the foundation of long-term success in real estate investing.

Chapter 15

The Ultimate Wealth Flywheel—Compounding Assets, Capital, and Control Over Time

At the highest level of real estate investing, everything begins to connect. What once felt like separate strategies—acquisition, financing, scaling, refinancing, and optimization—now merge into a single, powerful system. This system is what we call the wealth flywheel. It is the engine that transforms individual actions into compounding results, allowing foreign national investors to build extraordinary levels of wealth over time using asset-based mortgage strategies.

The concept of a flywheel is simple but profound. Instead of relying on isolated efforts to generate results, you create a system where each action reinforces the next. In real estate, this means using assets to acquire properties, properties to generate income, income to build reserves, reserves to support additional financing, and financing to acquire more assets. Over time, this cycle accelerates, creating momentum that becomes increasingly difficult to stop.

The first component of the wealth flywheel is capital. Capital is the starting point—it is what allows you to enter the system. For foreign national investors, this capital often exists in the form of global assets. Asset-based lending transforms these assets into actionable leverage, allowing you to acquire properties without relying on traditional income. This is the spark that initiates the flywheel.

The second component is acquisition. Each property you acquire becomes a new node in your system. It generates income, appreciates over time, and contributes to your overall portfolio. The key is to acquire strategically, focusing on properties that align with your long-term goals. Every acquisition should strengthen the flywheel, not disrupt it.

The third component is cash flow. Income generated from your properties fuels the system. It provides the liquidity needed to cover expenses, build reserves, and reinvest in new opportunities. Positive cash flow is not just a benefit—it is a requirement for sustainable growth. It ensures that your portfolio can support itself and continue expanding.

The fourth component is equity growth. As properties appreciate and loans are paid down, equity is created. This equity represents stored value that can be accessed and redeployed. Asset-based refinancing allows you to unlock this equity without selling your assets, providing additional capital for new acquisitions. The fifth component is reinvestment. Capital extracted from equity and income is reinvested into new opportunities, creating additional nodes in the system. This reinvestment is what drives compounding growth. Each cycle of the flywheel builds upon the last, increasing both scale and efficiency.

The sixth component is optimization. As the system grows, it must be refined and improved. This includes refinancing to reduce costs, upgrading properties to increase income, and reallocating capital to higher-performing assets. Optimization ensures that the flywheel operates at maximum efficiency.

The seventh component is control. At this stage, you are no longer reacting to the market—you are controlling your position within it. You have the ability to decide when to buy, when to refinance, and when to sell. This level of control is what allows you to navigate changing conditions and maintain momentum.

One of the most important aspects of the wealth flywheel is momentum. In the early stages, progress may feel slow. Each acquisition requires effort, and results may not be immediately visible. However, as the system grows, momentum builds. Income increases, equity compounds, and opportunities expand. Eventually, the flywheel reaches a point where growth becomes self-sustaining. Another key element is discipline. The flywheel only works if each component is managed effectively. Over-leveraging, poor acquisitions, or inadequate reserves can disrupt the system. Maintaining discipline ensures that the flywheel continues to operate smoothly and sustainably.

Time is the most powerful factor in this system. Compounding requires time to reach its full potential. Investors who remain consistent and patient are able to harness the full power of the flywheel. Those who seek quick results often miss the long-term benefits.

Foreign national investors have a unique advantage in building this system. Their ability to access global capital, diversify across markets, and leverage asset-based financing creates opportunities that are not available to many domestic investors. This global perspective enhances the effectiveness of the flywheel.

Another important concept is scalability. The flywheel is designed to grow. As more assets are added, the system becomes more powerful. However, scalability requires systems, partnerships, and infrastructure. Without these elements, growth can become chaotic and inefficient.

Risk management remains essential throughout the process. The flywheel should be built with resilience in mind. This includes maintaining reserves, diversifying assets, and avoiding excessive leverage. A resilient flywheel can withstand challenges and continue operating even during difficult conditions.

Legacy is the ultimate outcome of the wealth flywheel. Over time, the system creates not just income and assets, but a lasting financial structure that can be passed down and expanded. This transforms real estate investing from a personal endeavor into a generational strategy.

At this level, investing is no longer about individual deals—it is about managing and evolving a system. The wealth flywheel becomes the foundation of your financial life, driving growth, stability, and opportunity.

Real-Life Math Example: The Wealth Flywheel in Action Over Time

To illustrate how the wealth flywheel operates in practice, let us examine a detailed example of a foreign national investor building and accelerating this system over time.

Consider an investor named Rafael, based in Mexico, with $4,000,000 in qualifying assets. Rafael begins by allocating $1,200,000 for down payments, acquiring four properties with a combined value of $4,000,000. Each property requires a 30% down payment, resulting in a total loan amount of $2,800,000. These properties generate a combined rental income of $28,000 per month, with expenses of $20,000, resulting in a net cash flow of $8,000. Rafael reinvests this cash flow into his reserves and future acquisitions.

After two years, the properties appreciate to a combined value of $4,800,000. Rafael's loan balance decreases to $2,600,000, creating $2,200,000 in equity. He refinances at 70% loan-to-value, obtaining a new loan of $3,360,000. After paying off the existing loans, he extracts $760,000 in cash.

Rafael uses this capital, along with additional assets, to acquire three more properties valued at $3,000,000. His portfolio now includes seven properties with a total value of $7,800,000.

At this stage, his monthly rental income increases to $52,000, with expenses of $36,000, resulting in a net cash flow of $16,000. This increased income accelerates the flywheel, providing more capital for reinvestment.

Over the next three years, Rafael continues this cycle, acquiring additional properties, refinancing strategically, and reinvesting income. His portfolio grows to $15,000,000 in value, with a loan balance of $9,500,000 and equity of $5,500,000.

His monthly rental income reaches $95,000, with expenses of $60,000, resulting in a net cash flow of $35,000. The flywheel is now operating at full momentum, generating both income and equity at an accelerated rate. Rafael's system becomes self-sustaining. Income supports expenses, equity provides capital, and acquisitions drive growth. He no longer relies on external income—his portfolio generates the resources needed to continue expanding.

This example demonstrates the power of the wealth flywheel. By combining asset-based lending with disciplined strategy and reinvestment, Rafael transforms his initial capital into a dynamic and growing system.

As you move forward, remember that the flywheel is not built overnight. It requires patience, consistency, and strategic execution. But once it is in motion, it becomes one of the most powerful tools for building long-term wealth.

This is the ultimate goal—to create a system that works for you, grows with you, and sustains itself over time.

Final Thoughts

The Future You Build from Here

As you reach the end of this journey through foreign national asset-based mortgage lending, it is important to recognize that this is not an ending—it is a beginning. What you now possess is not just information, but a framework. A system. A new way of thinking about wealth, opportunity, and control. Throughout this book, you have moved from understanding the fundamentals to mastering advanced strategies, from seeing real estate as a transaction to seeing it as a scalable and evolving financial ecosystem. This shift in perspective is what separates those who participate from those who lead.

At its core, this entire strategy is built on a simple but powerful principle: your assets can work for you in ways that traditional systems often fail to recognize. You are no longer limited by income in one country, one job, or one currency. You are operating within a global framework where capital, opportunity, and strategy intersect. This is the true advantage of asset-based lending—it frees you from constraints and allows you to think and act on a larger scale.

But knowledge alone is not enough. The true value of what you have learned lies in execution. The strategies outlined in this book are only as powerful as your willingness to apply them.

This requires discipline, consistency, and a commitment to long-term thinking. Real estate is not a shortcut—it is a system that rewards patience and strategic action. Every decision you make, from your first acquisition to your long-term portfolio optimization, contributes to the foundation you are building.

One of the most important lessons to carry forward is the importance of clarity. Clarity in your goals, clarity in your strategy, and clarity in your execution. Without clarity, even the best opportunities can become distractions. With clarity, every step you take becomes intentional, aligned with a larger vision. This is what allows you to move forward with confidence, even in uncertain conditions.

Another key principle is control. Control over your assets, your financing, and your strategy. This does not mean eliminating risk, but rather understanding and managing it effectively. You have learned how to structure your assets, how to navigate lending requirements, and how to position yourself for approval and growth. This knowledge gives you control—not absolute certainty, but the ability to make informed decisions and adapt as needed.

Adaptability is essential in a world that is constantly changing. Markets will shift, interest rates will fluctuate, and new opportunities will emerge. The investors who succeed are not those who predict every change, but those who are prepared to respond. Asset-based lending provides the flexibility needed to adapt, allowing you to refinance, reposition, and reallocate as conditions evolve. This adaptability is one of your greatest strengths.

As you continue forward, remember that scaling is not about speed—it is about sustainability. Building a portfolio that grows too quickly without proper structure can create instability. On the other hand, a well-structured portfolio that grows steadily over time creates lasting value. Focus on building a system that supports growth, rather than chasing growth itself. This distinction is critical for long-term success.

The concept of leverage should also be approached with intention. Leverage is a tool, not a goal. It amplifies both opportunity and risk. When used strategically, it allows you to expand your portfolio and accelerate growth. When used carelessly, it can create vulnerability. The key is balance—using leverage to enhance your strategy while maintaining the stability needed to withstand challenges.

Another important takeaway is the role of systems. As your portfolio grows, your ability to manage it manually becomes limited. Systems—whether they involve processes, automation, or teams—allow you to operate efficiently and consistently.

They reduce complexity, improve performance, and free up your time to focus on higher-level decisions. Building systems is not optional—it is essential for scaling.

Your network will also play a significant role in your journey. Real estate is not a solo endeavor. It involves lenders, agents, property managers, legal advisors, and financial professionals. Building strong relationships with these individuals creates a support system that enhances your ability to execute. Choose your partners carefully, and invest in relationships that align with your goals.

As a foreign national investor, you have a unique advantage. You are not confined to a single market or financial system. You have the ability to operate globally, to allocate capital where it is most effective, and to diversify across borders. This perspective allows you to see opportunities that others may overlook. Embrace this advantage and use it to your benefit.

At the same time, remain mindful of the responsibilities that come with this level of opportunity. Compliance, transparency, and ethical practices are not just requirements—they are foundations for long-term success. By operating with integrity and clarity, you build trust with lenders, partners, and institutions, which in turn opens more doors. Legacy is another theme that should guide your thinking. The decisions you make today have the potential to impact not just your own future, but that of your family and future generations. Real estate, when structured and managed effectively, can become a lasting source of wealth and stability. Consider how your portfolio fits into a larger vision of generational impact.

It is also important to recognize that success is not linear. There will be challenges, setbacks, and moments of uncertainty. These are not signs of failure—they are part of the process. What matters is how you respond. The knowledge and strategies you have gained provide a framework for navigating these challenges with confidence and resilience.

As you move forward, continue to learn. The market evolves, and so should your strategy. Stay informed, seek out new insights, and remain open to innovation. The most successful investors are those who never stop refining their approach.

Finally, take a moment to recognize what you have accomplished by reaching this point. You have invested time and effort into understanding a complex and powerful system. You have developed a perspective that goes beyond traditional limitations. You are now equipped with the tools to build, scale, and optimize a real estate portfolio using asset-based strategies.

The next step is yours. The opportunities are real. The strategies are proven. The framework is in place.

What you build from here will depend on your vision, your discipline, and your willingness to act.

This is not the end of your journey.

It is the beginning of everything that comes next.

How to Get a Personalized Asset-Based Mortgage Review

If you found this book helpful, you may want to see how these concepts apply to your specific financial situation. Asset-based lending is highly customized—your assets, liquidity, credit profile, property type, and long-term goals all play a role in determining what you qualify for and how your loan should be structured.

Every borrower's situation is different. The type of assets you hold, how those assets are allocated, your credit history, the property you are purchasing or refinancing, and current lender guidelines all affect your options. The strategies and examples in this book are designed to teach you how asset-based mortgage loans work—but your actual qualifying income, loan amount, and structure can only be determined by reviewing your real numbers.

If you would like a no-obligation Asset-Based Mortgage review, you can request one here:

Email: **info@FinibiMortgage.com**

A licensed mortgage broker will review your assets, credit profile, and goals, and explain what asset-based mortgage options may be available to you—including asset depletion loans, investment property financing, refinancing strategies, and advanced structuring approaches tailored to your situation.

No cost. No pressure. No obligation.

Sincerely,

Joseph G. Correa

About the Author

Joseph G. Correa is a licensed mortgage broker and the founder of Finibi Mortgage, a Florida-based brokerage specializing in asset-based mortgage lending, alternative financing, and strategic real estate funding solutions for homeowners, investors, and high-net-worth borrowers. With more than two decades of experience in mortgage lending, underwriting, and financial structuring, Joseph has helped thousands of clients qualify for real estate using assets instead of traditional income, unlocking opportunities that conventional lending often restricts.

Unlike traditional loan officers who focus solely on income-based approvals, Joseph's approach is centered on asset positioning, financial strategy, and long-term wealth building. He believes that mortgages should not be limited by outdated income rules, but instead structured around true financial strength—assets, liquidity, and intelligent leverage. This philosophy has made him a trusted advisor for entrepreneurs, retirees, self-employed individuals, and investors who need flexible financing solutions that align with how they actually build and manage wealth.

Joseph is widely recognized for his expertise in asset depletion mortgage loans, bank statement programs, non-QM lending, investment property financing, and advanced structuring strategies that allow borrowers to qualify without relying on tax returns or W-2 income. His ability to simplify complex underwriting guidelines into clear, actionable strategies has helped clients use their savings, investment portfolios, and retirement accounts to acquire real estate, scale portfolios, and preserve liquidity.

Through his education platform, Finibi Academy, Joseph has trained tens of thousands of students worldwide in mortgage strategy, credit optimization, real estate investing, and financial independence. His courses and books are designed for both beginners and experienced professionals who want a deeper understanding of how modern lending truly works beyond traditional income-based limitations.

Joseph created The Asset-Based Mortgage Mastery Series to provide a clear, practical roadmap for borrowers and professionals who want to leverage assets instead of income to qualify for real estate. His mission is simple: to help people understand how to use their assets as a powerful financial tool, eliminate unnecessary barriers to financing, and build long-term wealth through strategic lending.

When he is not structuring loans or writing, Joseph works with clients across the United States to design customized asset-based mortgage strategies that align with their financial goals, liquidity needs, and long-term investment plans.

The Asset-Based Mortgage Mastery Series Roadmap

The Professional Guide to Qualifying for Real Estate Using Assets, Not Income

The purpose of *The Asset-Based Mortgage Mastery Series* is to give borrowers, investors, and financial professionals the same strategies used by banks, private lenders, and institutional investors—translated into clear, practical guidance that can be applied in real life. This series is designed to take you from foundational understanding to advanced mastery of how to qualify for, structure, and scale real estate financing using assets instead of traditional income.

Each book builds on the last. You are not just learning how to get approved—you are learning how to think, structure, and operate like the institutions that control capital.

Book 1 — Asset-Based Mortgage Loan Fundamentals
This book gives you the foundation. You will understand how asset-based mortgage loans work, how asset depletion is calculated, how lenders evaluate risk, and why income is no longer the only path to qualification. This is where you shift your mindset from income-based borrowing to asset-based strategy.

Book 2 — Retirement Asset Mortgage Qualification
This book focuses on using retirement accounts such as

401(k)s, IRAs, and investment portfolios to qualify for mortgage loans. You will learn how lenders evaluate retirement assets, how to access them strategically, and how to structure your finances to qualify without disrupting long-term retirement growth.

Book 3 — High-Net-Worth Asset-Based Mortgage Strategies

This book is designed for borrowers with significant assets who want to optimize leverage, preserve liquidity, and structure large or complex transactions. You will learn how wealthy borrowers qualify without traditional income and how to position assets for maximum efficiency and control.

Book 4 — Primary Residence Asset-Based Mortgage Loans

This book shows you how to purchase or refinance your primary home using assets instead of income. You will learn how to structure down payments, reserves, and loan options to maximize flexibility while maintaining long-term financial stability.

Book 5 — Investment Property Asset-Based Mortgage Loans

This book focuses on building a real estate portfolio using asset-based lending. You will learn how to qualify for multiple properties, integrate rental income, manage reserves, and scale your investments without being limited by income.

Book 6 — Securities-Based Mortgage Lending Strategies

This book explores how to use stocks, bonds, and brokerage accounts to secure financing. You will learn how to leverage investment portfolios without liquidating them, preserving growth while accessing capital for real estate opportunities.

Book 7 — Foreign National Asset-Based Mortgage Loans

This book explains how international buyers can qualify for U.S. real estate using global assets. You will learn how lenders evaluate foreign income and assets, and how to structure deals across borders with confidence.

Book 8 — Jumbo Asset-Based Mortgage Loans

This book focuses on financing high-value and luxury properties. You will learn how to structure large loan amounts, meet stricter guidelines, and position assets to qualify for jumbo financing without traditional income.

Book 9 — Asset-Based Mortgage Refinancing & Equity Access

This book teaches you how to unlock equity from existing properties using asset-based strategies. You will learn how to refinance without income, access liquidity, and use your equity to fund new investments or opportunities.

Book 10 — Advanced Asset-Based Mortgage Structuring

This book brings everything together. You will learn how to engineer approvals, layer assets, sequence transactions, and create sophisticated financing strategies that maximize flexibility, control, and long-term growth.

This series is designed to move you step-by-step from understanding to execution to mastery. By the end, you will not just know how to qualify for loans—you will understand how to control capital, structure wealth, and build a financial system that works for you long-term.

Educational & Financial Disclaimer

The *Asset-Based Mortgage Mastery Series* is intended for educational and informational purposes only. The content provided throughout this series is designed to help readers better understand asset-based mortgage lending, real estate financing strategies, and financial structuring concepts. It is not intended to be, and should not be interpreted as, financial, legal, tax, investment, or mortgage advice.

Joseph G. Correa and Live Stronger Faster are not acting as your personal financial advisor, attorney, accountant, or licensed mortgage professional in any jurisdiction through this publication. All information is presented in a general format and may not apply to your specific financial situation, goals, or circumstances. Readers are strongly encouraged to consult with qualified professionals—including licensed mortgage brokers, financial advisors, tax professionals, and attorneys—before making any financial or real estate decisions.

Mortgage lending guidelines, underwriting standards, and loan program availability vary by lender, location, and over time. Asset-based mortgage programs, including asset depletion loans and non-qualified mortgage (Non-QM) products, are subject to change without notice. The examples, strategies, and scenarios presented in this series are for illustration purposes only and do not guarantee approval, specific loan terms, or financial outcomes. Individual results will vary based on credit profile, asset structure, property type, market conditions, and lender requirements.

Real estate investing and the use of leverage involve risk. Property values can fluctuate, interest rates can change, and market conditions may impact both income and asset performance. While asset-based lending provides flexibility, it also requires careful planning, risk management, and financial discipline. Readers are responsible for evaluating their own risk tolerance and making decisions that align with their long-term financial goals.

Any references to potential income, returns, cash flow, or financial growth are not guarantees or promises of performance. These outcomes depend on multiple factors beyond the control of the author and publisher, including economic conditions, market trends, borrower decisions, and lender policies.

The author and publisher make no representations or warranties regarding the accuracy, completeness, or reliability of the information contained in this series. While every effort has been made to provide accurate and up-to-date information, errors or omissions may occur. The author and publisher disclaim any liability for losses, damages, or consequences resulting from the use or misuse of the information provided.

By reading this series, you acknowledge that you are solely responsible for your financial decisions and actions. The purpose of this content is to provide knowledge, perspective, and strategic insight—not to replace professional advice or guarantee specific outcomes.

Use this information as a guide, not a substitute for professional consultation, and always make decisions based on your individual financial situation, goals, and risk tolerance.

Risk Disclosure

The *Asset-Based Mortgage Mastery Series* discusses financial strategies involving real estate, lending, leverage, and asset-based qualification methods. These strategies involve inherent risks, and it is important that all readers fully understand and accept these risks before applying any concepts presented in this series.

Real estate markets are subject to fluctuation. Property values may rise or fall due to economic conditions, interest rate changes, local market dynamics, or unforeseen events. There is no guarantee that any property will appreciate in value or generate consistent income. Investments in real estate may result in financial loss.

The use of leverage, including mortgage financing and asset-based lending, increases both potential returns and potential risks. Borrowing against assets or property can amplify losses if market conditions change or if income from investments does not perform as expected. Failure to meet loan obligations may result in foreclosure, loss of property, or damage to credit.

Asset-based mortgage lending relies on the valuation and accessibility of financial assets. Investment accounts, retirement funds, and other assets may fluctuate in value due to market volatility. A decline in asset value may impact a borrower's financial position, liquidity, and ability to refinance or secure additional financing.

Interest rates may change over time, particularly with adjustable-rate or interest-only loan structures. Rising interest rates can increase monthly payments, reduce cash flow, and affect long-term affordability. Borrowers must be prepared for potential payment increases and plan accordingly.

Liquidity risk is another important consideration. While asset-based lending allows borrowers to qualify using assets, those assets may be tied up in investments or subject to penalties or restrictions. In times of financial stress, accessing funds may not be as immediate or favorable as expected.

Rental income and investment returns are not guaranteed. Vacancy, tenant issues, maintenance costs, property management expenses, and market conditions can all impact cash flow. Relying on projected income without accounting for these variables can create financial strain.

Refinancing and equity access strategies depend on market conditions, property values, and lender guidelines. There is no assurance that refinancing will be available in the future or that favorable terms will be offered. Changes in lending standards or economic conditions may limit access to capital.

Private lending, capital recycling, and advanced financial strategies discussed in this series involve additional layers of risk, including borrower default, insufficient collateral, and market uncertainty. These strategies require careful due diligence and risk management.

Tax laws and regulations may change over time, affecting the benefits of certain strategies such as depreciation, capital gains deferral, or asset structuring. Readers should consult with qualified tax professionals to understand how these changes may impact their financial plans.

All financial decisions involve risk, and past performance or examples presented in this series do not guarantee future results. The scenarios and illustrations provided are for educational purposes only and may not reflect actual outcomes. Individual results will vary based on personal circumstances, market conditions, and execution.

By using the information in this series, you acknowledge that you understand the risks involved and accept full responsibility for your financial decisions. The author and publisher are not liable for any losses, damages, or outcomes resulting from the application of the concepts discussed.

It is essential to approach asset-based lending and real estate investing with careful planning, professional guidance, and a clear understanding of your financial goals and risk tolerance.

www.ingramcontent.com/pod-product-compliance
Lightning Source LLC
LaVergne TN
LVHW022221200926
848481LV00006B/2066